# THE HIGH COST OF PREJUDICE

# THE
# HIGH COST
## OF
# PREJUDICE

*by*

## BUCKLIN MOON

**NEGRO UNIVERSITIES PRESS**
WESTPORT, CONNECTICUT

Reprinted by permission
of Julian Messner, Inc.,
A Division of Simon & Schuster, Inc., New York

Reprinted in 1970 by
Negro Universities Press
A Division of Greenwood Press, Inc.
Westport, Connecticut

Library of Congress Catalogue Card Number 70-111584

SBN 8371-4608-9

Printed in the United States of America

*FOR*
*JONATHAN*

# ACKNOWLEDGMENT

AS I LOOK back, I realize that this is hardly my book at all. Actually neither idea nor title was mine, both being generously suggested by Franklin Watts, who also gave me every encouragement. To him I owe a debt that I can hardly repay.

Further, if I were to acknowledge by name every person who helped in gathering the background material the list might be longer than the book itself. Since this is not feasible I want to take this opportunity to offer blanket thanks to everyone who was kind enough to answer my plea for suggestions.

But there were others with whom I had the opportunity to talk personally and all were unsparing with their time. To Sterling A. Brown, then, Roi Ottley, Henry Lee Moon, E. Franklin Frazier, and especially Horace R. Cayton, my special thanks. I am also deeply indebted to Dr. Charles S. Johnson, president of Fisk University, for the generous invitation to spend a week at the Institution of Race Relations, which verified some of my own thinking and gave me a deeper insight into things I had missed along the way. Lastly to the Rosenwald Fund—Edwin Embree, Dr. Will W. Alexander and Billy and Vandi Haygood in particular—I owe a debt of long standing.

I hope I have forgotten no one. If I have, put it down to the rather hectic conditions under which I am forced to work. But I am deeply grateful to all, for without their help this book could never have been completed.

BUCKLIN MOON

# CONTENTS

# INTRODUCTION

THERE IS nothing new about prejudice. The chances are that it has existed for as long a time as man has inhabited the face of the earth. Before we advanced into civilization man lived mainly by hunting and fishing. At first, while game was still plentiful, he had little fear of losing his means of livelihood; when he remained too long in one spot, however, game thinned out and before long the area was barely capable of supporting those already there. The moment that strangers moved in the feeling of security of those native to the area was immediately challenged.

If the natives happened to have black hair and that of the strangers was red, a new thought process was set up in underdeveloped minds. From that point on men with red hair were always identified as greedy and not to be trusted. Moreover, those responsible for this theory passed it on to all other black-haired men, not as mere superstition but as established fact, supported by all kinds of legends palmed off as personal experience. It was not long before all men with black hair believed it, and the legend had become an integral part of the culture of all dark-haired peoples.

Possibly there was a slight variation to this incident. Let us assume that the red-haired men were outnumbered, which could have caused a different kind of myth. Hunting and fishing had grown so difficult that they were no longer enjoyable tasks. Into the minds of the physically superior came a new notion. Here were likely candidates for hunting and fishing; if it were possible to feed them less than they were capable of producing, there would be a net gain to the community. It seems doubtful that man at this early stage of his development had much of a sense of right and wrong; but if he did, new stuff could always be spun from the folklore in order to justify his position. See, he might say, these poor, misguided savages came to us without a pelt on their backs. They were weak and in need of our help. They have received the benefits of our superior way of life.

At first this may have been a little difficult for even black-haired men to believe, for the chances are that the new slaves were far from docile and did not take too kindly to their bondage. Some ungratefully ran away, and it became necessary to keep a close watch on them, even to the extent of locking them in a rough stockade at night. By day they were hobbled with thongs which made it possible for them to move around for purposes of work, yet kept them from straying too far away to be rounded up once again when the sun went down. At times it was even necessary to get a little rough and mete out punishment so that they would retain the proper feeling of inferior beings. It was not long before a system was worked out which seemed to function as well as could be expected. Once in a while an individual slave escaped, or several rose up and fought it out with their oppressors, yet so long as the majority were kept under control all seemed well.

Soon the dark-haired peoples found that their myth had

become fact. The slaves *were* docile and content in captivity, inferior beings who wanted nothing more of life than they received under slavery. Furthermore whatever it was that dark-haired men worshiped had looked down from above and found what they were doing had a moral justification. How such a conclusion was reached matters' little, for word from above must always be interpreted by mere man. Eventually our little society blossomed into a full civilization, replete with an economy, a legend and a fierce pride that it was the most golden of all civilizations.

This is, of course, an oversimplification and one might think that it has little application to the world of today. After all man has progressed in the years since he was a semi-savage trying to wrest his living from the virgin forest by hunting and fishing. As he advanced up the ladder of evolution, it would seem that he would have outgrown such foolishness. Today man is capable of reason and he has harnessed the laws of nature to work for him; yet prejudice and discrimination are still with us.

Why? For one thing, as man has progressed his life has become more complex. Mastery of the machine has meant a compromise in turn with the simplicity with which man once made a living and this, if anything, has increased his feeling of insecurity. New tensions have arisen. Where once new frontiers seemed endless, now there are none; the world has grown more static and no longer can a man, when he grows tired of the thrust of competition around him, throw his belongings into a wagon and strike out for virgin territory.

Man has created a wonderful collection of machinery which is awesome to look upon; it would seem that there is nothing under the sun that it cannot do. The trouble is that every now and then it breaks down and refuses to function. Suddenly man, who has created this phenomenon and should by all rights be able to control it, finds that this is not necessarily the case. Being human—and somewhat of a fraud in the bargain—his first reaction is to blame someone else, to find a scapegoat in order to maintain his supremacy.

In the case of Hitler's Germany that scapegoat, as we all know, was the Jew. In fact Hitler sold the world the legend of Jewish guilt so well that, in a recent survey among American occupation troops stationed in Germany, twenty-two per cent answered that Hitler had good reason for his persecution of the Jews and an additional ten per cent were "undecided." Many whites in our own South feel that the Negro is the chief reason for their woes and some people on the West Coast believe there is actually a yellow peril in their midst.

But it is in his individual life where man is most prejudiced. The daily competition seems so intense that each time he sees someone who is different from himself he feels a direct threat to his own existence. He mutters to himself that if the "niggers" didn't have all the jobs a white man might have a chance, or if the "kikes" didn't control all the money he might be able to get more of it for himself.

Man, because of his lack of security, has developed an inferiority complex and like most people who have inferiority complexes he likes to brag about himself and say that his country, or his particular part of the country, is the best in the world and that anyone who differs from him in any way is an inferior person. On the group level this is Nationalism, of course, and we recognize its dangers; yet many of us are smugly guilty of the same thing on the individual level. Even though we may not actually discriminate against others who differ from us, we seldom think of them as our equals.

At first glance this may seem logical. It might even appear that those who practice prejudice and discrimination gain by it. But if this gain exists, which is debatable, it exists only for the short haul. Actually, one important facet of prejudice is not its effect on those who are discriminated against but on those who perpetrate such bias. It makes itself felt in three ways—financially, in a loss of efficiency, and in a general as well as personal corruption.

The purpose of this book is to examine these costs in some of the areas where they most frequently appear. To do so we shall examine most carefully prejudice and discrimination against the Negro. The reason for this is that the treatment of the Negro in America might well be termed the common denominator of all discrimination. Although Negroes have been in America for over three hundred years, they are still treated as foreign. Yet the Negro's ties with Africa are considerably less than those which any other minority group has with the country of its origin. There are no language ties and few if any customs have been carried over into his life here. Aside from a feeling of sympathy towards Ethiopia, when that little country was ravished by Italy, or the temporary magnetic impact generated by a Marcus Garvey, few Negroes have any feelings one way or another about Africa. Yet, in this respect, Negroes are often treated as though they sprang fresh out of the jungle last Saturday night.

In part, the Negro suffers hardest from discrimination because of his high rate of visibility. A dark skin is easily picked out in a crowd, a hardship Negroes share, to an extent, with some other minorities such as Mexicans and Orientals. Being our largest minority group, the Negro becomes in a sense the barometer of discrimination. In areas where Negroes are badly treated, other minority groups likewise have a hard time of it—not as hard to be sure, but their sufferings are nonetheless in ratio. Where Negroes are less badly treated, other minorities usually have a better time of it. This is not always the case but usually it is. Thus we shall be applying our yardstick most often to his environment, showing by such measurements the indirect effect on all minorities.

Actually the Negro has played the same tragic rôle in America that the Jew played in Nazi Germany. True, even in our most prejudiced areas it has been a similarity of quality rather than quantity, yet the applications have been the same. We know something of the effect which this had had on the Negro, but we have thought too little about the implications in regard to ourselves.

Man is a creature of habit and his prejudices are a part of him not too easily shaken. A young novelist, Robert Bright, puts his finger on the problem when he has one of his characters * say: "The inferiority of the Negro is not a fact, it is a faith for which some men are willing to give their lives." Too often we have taken in racism with our

---

* *The Intruders* by Robert Bright. Doubleday.

mother's milk, and it is buried deep within us all. Social pressures in the community are often strong. It is not the easiest thing in the world to go against them, though many do. But most important is that those symbols which control the community—the church, the press, the better people and the business interests—are firmly opposed to any change in the status quo.

One fact is ever present and that is the unpleasant truth that the forces of prejudice are on the upsurge in spite of our rather futile efforts to combat them. This is not limited to any region, or to any one minority. There is more anti-Semitism in today's America than there has ever been before. Nor is the South the only place where one finds violent anti-Negro sentiments, a fact too many Northern liberals completely ignore. The zoot suit riots in Los Angeles left a lasting impression on California thinking in relationship to the Mexican American; and the forced evacuation of all Japanese from the West Coast, regardless of citizenship or loyalty, is indicative of another form of prejudice. Even religious minorities come in for a share of this baiting.

Where is all this leading us as a nation? Certainly not in the direction of a unified America. The Negro problem, in a different form, split us tragically once; will this, or another minority problem, again drive a wedge between Americans? More probable is the possibility that increased feelings against minorities may drive us into a pattern not too different from Nazi Germany, for the same seeds are already planted here. That they have not thus far taken deep root does not rule out the possibility of their eventually doing so.

# INTRODUCTION

What, then, is the answer? It is obvious that we must stop thinking only in terms of tolerance or of race relations, and think in terms of a solution. The Negro problem, or any minority problem, is not, as some have led us to believe, insoluble. But to solve it we must use every available weapon. The purpose of this book is to look at the problem from a different angle. This writer knows that there is a high cost involved in prejudice, but he also knows that no one person can gather together the undeniable proof into a neat series of charts and graphs. Such a project will, I hope, some day be financed to the extent necessary to produce scientific results. So far as I have been able to discover there are no such statistics available now and this book will not furnish them, though it will show where they might be discovered.

If this book is not the best possible book on the subject, I can only plead that so far as I know it is the first, and, within the limitations of time and available data, I am not ashamed of it.

BUCKLIN MOON

NEW YORK, N. Y.
August, 1946

# THE HIGH COST OF PREJUDICE

## CHAPTER ONE

# TEST TUBE OF RACIAL DISCRIMINATION

THE SOUTH might well be called the test tube of racial discrimination since it is the only area in America where such discrimination is practiced *by* law rather than *in spite of* it. It is not within the province of this book to give detailed consideration to how the South got that way. Our only interest is to find out if there is any relationship between the racial mores of the South and the fact that the region has been called the No. 1 Economic Problem of the nation.* Is this only because of freight differentials, absentee ownership and lack of local capital? Or is it also because in order to keep the Negro in his place you have to get down in the gutter with him?

It has been said that the South is more a state of mind than a geographical area—another way of saying that the basis of most Southern thinking is to be found in a legend. That legend was created many years ago and repeated so often that for a time we in the North came to believe in it as fully as most Southerners. Until very recently, in fact, it was an integral part of our nationwide racial thinking. It was reflected in our literature, drama and songs—in our whole folklore.

---

* By President Roosevelt after studying the report of the National Emergency Council in 1938.

3

# THE HIGH COST OF PREJUDICE

This Southern legend can be stated in a few words. After Reconstruction laid low the whole South, the Negro was forced into a competition where he was unable to hold his own, because he was an inferior being incapable of absorbing an education or learning the know-how of a mechanized civilization. Since he was a happy and child-like person, lazy by nature, sexually dangerous and latently criminal, it was necessary for the white South to take care of him, because only a Southerner could really understand Negroes.

More recently, we in the North have begun to realize the fallacy in this reasoning, mainly through necessity, however, and not moral indignation. The Negro worker during the war demonstrated his mastery of the machine and also proved himself as a soldier. He has shown an aptitude for learning which in no way differs from our own, and scientists have effectively spiked the falseness in the reasoning that he is any different physically. Lillian Smith, a white Southerner, has said quite rightly that there is no longer a Negro problem but in reality a white problem. In other words, if the white man would get up off the Negro's neck and give him equal opportunity, what little remains of the problem would be solved by rapid evolution.

But this the white Southerner, and to some extent the white Northerner, has thus far been unwilling to do. Instead, he keeps on repeating that the Negro is a problem, meanwhile continuing to do everything possible to keep Negroes in the position of second-class citizenship which makes it difficult for them to be anything else. In short, the Negro is a problem which the white South has created and intends to perpetuate. Is it worth it for the white South to

4

go on paying the price which the maintenance of that problem makes necessary?

Few Southerners agree that this is true, claiming that they are the best friend the Negro has, and that, within the pattern of segregation, the South is doing everything possible to help him in every way. This process, usually referred to as "Separate but Equal," to a large extent stems historically from a speech delivered by the Negro leader, Booker T. Washington, at the Atlanta Exposition on September 18, 1895. At a dramatic point in his plea for better opportunities for Negroes in the South, Washington said: "In all things purely social we can be as separate as the fingers, yet one as the hand in all things essential to human progress." Washington's hope for a platform upon which "whites and blacks could stand with full justice to each other" was never realized; rather his speech was a signal for the tightening of jim crow restrictions all over the South.

It seems fairly obvious that the South betrayed Booker T. Washington, but did it not betray itself as well? True, it created a nice-sounding slogan, but close examination shows it to be as meaningless as most slogans. For example, it has been estimated that eighty per cent of all Negroes in the South fall into the lowest of income brackets, while less than twenty-five per cent of the white group finds itself in such a low income stratum. At the other end of the scale, moreover, eighteen per cent of the white population will earn more than $2000 in a normal year, while a mere tenth of one per cent of the colored population can hope to do as well.

5

# THE HIGH COST OF PREJUDICE

It is sometimes possible to put up with extreme hardship if one knows that through a better education one's children will be able to advance themselves. Yet in 1942 there was one school for every 855 white children in Atlanta as against one for every 2,040 colored children. The same city was willing to spend $108.70 to educate a white child, but only $37.80 for each Negro pupil.

This sounds more like separate and *unequal.* In fact, is it possible to have equality within the pattern of segregation? It would mean an exact duplication of the existing transportation facilities, a dual school system including an adequate university set-up, and the equalization of all wage levels and public housing, to mention only the more obvious and costly. There are no estimates available on what this actually would cost, but certainly an economy already near subsistence levels could hardly withstand the shock. The only other alternative would be to lower white levels to compensate for the existing inequalities and it seems doubtful that the South, even to retain its policy of complete segregation, would agree to a further lowering of its already low standard of living.

What the jim crow pattern has done to the Negro is fairly well documented, but what of its effect on the white Southerner? A public hearing was recently held in Durham, North Carolina, to discuss the need for raising the Minimum Wage Act from forty to sixty-five cents, with an increase to seventy cents in two years, and an additional hike to seventy-five cents by 1950. The testimony of a white textile worker, a recently discharged war veteran, showed that as a private in the army, plus allotments, he had been considerably better off financially than he now was working in a Southern cotton mill. The same is largely true in the other two important industries in the South, tobacco and lumber. Yet all three have enjoyed large profits and could well afford a wage increase.

Southern industry, in the geographic sense, has long enjoyed an over-supply of docile, white labor by holding over its head the threat of throwing the Negro, at even lower wages, into direct competition. Largely unorganized until recently, white labor in the South has often resisted unionization, which would better its condition, because management has skillfully played on racial prejudice by intimating that unions would bring social equality. The war years have modified this pattern, but management still hopefully is trying to play the same game.

One field in which the South can little afford a loss in revenue is education. In the year 1935–36 estimates show that ten Northern states had an average educational expenditure of $104.47 per pupil, as against a figure of $33.16 for ten Southern states. Nor do these figures show the whole picture. Actually the Southern states levy a higher percentage of tax for schooling than do the Northern states. Yet shortly after these same years, when a bill was introduced to provide federal aid to counterbalance this discrepancy, it was killed by the representatives of these same Southern states because the funds to be made available were not earmarked jim crow! White supremacy is indeed a costly luxury.

Actually, "keeping the Negro in his place" by not paying him decent wages has another effect on the Southern economy, though it is difficult to arrive at a dollars and cents evaluation. However, some interesting deductions can be

7

drawn. New York's 458,000 Negroes, for example, spent five-sevenths of their income in 1943 for local consumer goods and services. A little simple arithmetic shows the potential value of the Negro market in the South, if earning power were only slightly increased.

The South has always justified its inequalities toward the Negro by the claim that Negroes paid little in taxes to support such public facilities. This happens to be true and for obvious reasons. There are no readily accessible comparisons between revenue collected from white and colored taxpayers; but since the region is so badly in need of additional revenue, it would seem that one way to get it would be to equalize white and Negro wage levels.

Federal Bureau of Investigations figures show that the South leads all other areas in murder, including non-negligent manslaughter, aggravated assault and burglary. Figures on crime in the South are in many respects meaningless, for a reason which is an integral part of racial mores. Deep-seated in the regional practices of inequality is a rather complex and little understood method of handing out punitive measures. If a Negro commits homicide against a white, his chances for acquittal are slight and he runs the added risk of mob violence. On the other hand, if his victim happens to be another Negro, his chances of getting off are better than average. Even if he is found guilty, his sentence will be light, out of all proportion to the crime he has committed. The same is true of homicide charges against whites.

The costly effect of this can easily be seen. Violence among both whites and Negroes is the rule rather than the exception, hardly a healthy situation. Another segment of the same picture which is not always understood is the fact that in many areas of the South feeble-mindedness, and sometimes actual insanity, is not deemed of sufficient importance, when it occurs among Negroes, to call for preventive measures. The relationship between this and the potentially criminal is obvious, though it in no sense implies that the Negro is any more latently criminal than any other group.

Perhaps, however, the greatest loss that the South suffers from its racial attitudes is in efficiency. It appears on many levels, one of them a hangover from the master-slave relationship which created caste taboos toward certain kinds of work. At its worst it meant that there were many types of jobs which no man with a white skin would touch, even though his children were starving, because they were known as "Negro" jobs. The belief that menial work was degrading was modified in the last depression, when whites took over many work areas where Negroes had formerly had what amounted to a monopoly. But even more important, when a whole civilization is built and maintained on a too cheap supply of black labor, it is bound to be sapped of some of its inherent stamina and ambition.

On another level—the lawful carrying out of jim crow policies—one sees plainly the inconveniences to which most white Southerners must subject themselves in order to maintain their doubtful supremacy. In these past few years transportation facilities have become so overcrowded that normal travel has become a nightmare and is likely

9

to remain so for some time. If one adds to this the difficulty of maintaining jim crow seating arrangements, the nightmare assumes even more gigantic proportions.

This is especially true on busses. Briefly, jim crow works this way: the rear of the bus is reserved for Negroes, the front for whites. The reason for this, supposedly, is to maintain as rigid a separation as possible between the races. In theory this may be true, but actually the reverse often happens. Because such conveyances load from the front and usually unload the same way, there is, if anything, even closer contact. Negroes getting into a crowded bus must force their way to the rear and the same, in reverse, is often true when they get off. Multiply this all over the South and one gets a little insight into the physical discomfort involved. The lengths to which whites must go in order to maintain this quasi-separation seem hardly worth the effort.

Nor are many of the same physical discomforts absent from train travel. The old formula of giving Negroes lower 13 (a drawing room for the price of a lower) when it was impossible to deny them Pullman accommodations, was never economically feasible and is impossible in this day of shortages. The segregation of Negro diners at the two end tables of dining cars and shutting them off by green curtains, also creates complications. If no Negro happens to be in the dining car such restrictions are not, of course, carried out, and the curtains remain unobtrusively pulled aside. Yet let one lone colored diner appear, and five unoccupied seats at the two tables become unavailable for any hungry white. Seeing perhaps two dozen people who have been standing in line for half an hour suddenly by-passed by a Negro, one wonders how many of those tired Nordics might be willing to change places with him—if the laws of the sovereign state through which the train was passing allowed them to do so.

The railroads are not at fault.* They are only following the directives of state laws. But those who scan dining-car receipts must be weary of seeing where one colored diner can tie up five empty places, which means the loss of the sale of five additional meals.

There are numerous other examples of the inefficiency and the inconveniences which are part and parcel of jim crow. All of them are by no means limited to the South. But wherever they exist, lawfully or by subterfuge, they are a costly business.

The psychological impact upon those who practice prejudice is also costly. White Southerners are fond of saying that there is no Negro problem, that if the damyankees would just leave the Negro alone, all would be serene and without friction. Yet the extent to which the Negro dominates conversation in Dixie is a dead giveaway. This was humorously demonstrated in a story reported by Ray Stannard Baker almost a generation ago.

A young Negro boy went into domestic service in the home of a prominent white family in Atlanta. His family, naturally curious about the goings on in the big house, began to query him one day.

---

* Recently Rule T18 of the Alabama Public Service Commission, which would have further strengthened jim crow restrictions on trains, was defeated by the railroads as being too expensive of execution.

"What do they talk about?" they asked him.

The boy thought a moment, then replied, "Well, mostly they discusses us colored folks."

The South has not changed to this day in that respect. In the last few years stories about mythical Eleanor Clubs, Negro uprisings during trial blackouts, and rumors about what the Negro service man planned to do when he returned to the South, have swept the region. But these are only symptoms of something which goes far deeper, the need to justify clinging to outmoded ways of thinking, itself the result of a feeling of guilt. Even the most self-assured Southerner realizes that somehow all is not as it should be. America fought a war to do away with racial discriminations not too different from those practiced in the South. If Nazi treatment of the Jew was wrong, then can all be right in the Kingdom of jim crow?

A Rankin or a Bilbo insists that white supremacy is morally right and segregation must not be weakened by so much as one link. Many white Southerners deny that such men speak for the region, though actually they seem unwilling to do a great deal about freeing the area from such demagogues. A Virginius Dabney or a Mark Ethridge, on the other hand, may admit that jim crow is not right; yet they as stoutly maintain that any rapid attempt to break down segregation will only bring violence down upon the heads of those least able to withstand it, Negroes themselves. However there are straws in the wind that make one doubt if this is altogether true.

In fact some signs seem to point in the opposite direction. For one thing the mores of the South have changed in the past five years. Such modifications taken singly may not seem important, but added together they show at least a trend. These changes include a lessening of the use of courtesy titles, a different racial etiquette in shopping lines, and the appearance of Negroes in places where they have not been usually seen. Even occasionally the jim crow pattern in the border states has been challenged—not always successfully, but once in a while without incident. There has been a great deal of talk and some violence, but it is interesting to note that at least one barometer of that violence went down and stayed down until fanned by demagogues in the recent primary elections in Mississippi and Georgia. In 1942, when the reaction against change was probably at its peak, there were five lynchings in the United States, all in the South. But what happened in the years that followed? Although they could not be properly termed periods when tensions and pressures on the part of Negroes and liberals for change lessened, there were only three lynchings in 1943, and two in 1944.

It would be wrong to deduce from this that the problem of prejudice and discrimination in the South is well on its way to a rapid solution. The most optimistic interpretation possible is merely that cracks are beginning to show on the surface. The Bilboes and the Rankins still filibuster successfully against a permanent FEPC, apparently with the full approval of their constituents. Yet the white South is no longer sure of its position and it is far from at ease. "Would you want your sister to marry a Negro?" no longer answers all racial arguments; but, lacking progressive leadership, the white South does little more than go on repeat-

13

ing the old shibboleths, hollow as they are beginning to sound to many Southern ears.

The moral corruption of jim crow is as plain to see in the South as it was in Nazi Germany, and on as many levels. Some Southerners have been brutalized; it shows in their faces and in their actions. Others have leaned too heavily on the unstable prop that no matter how low a white man may sink, he is still better than a Negro. This, after all, is the one justification for the ignorance, poverty and moral impotence of many whites. Intellectually it has blinded a great many Southerners to any social progress, no matter how beneficial it might be. Lastly, a great many people who are normally decent and want to see a better break for *all* peoples, regardless of race, creed or color, are bewildered. They flounder about in the past, carrying with them a guilt feeling which is the price they must pay for jim crow.

Ralph Barton Perry once wrote: "The good of any man, or the satisfaction of any interest of any man, is dependent on the goods and satisfaction of every other man."

14

## CHAPTER TWO

# *LAST TO BE HIRED; FIRST TO BE FIRED*

LAST TO be hired and first to be fired has always made any sort of economic stability difficult for the Negro. It has made security difficult for other minorities as well. Industry has exploited this situation whenever possible, which has tended to place a ceiling on wages and drive pay checks downward. So long as there is a large reservior of labor which can be utilized at a lower economic level, this threat can be used to hold in check the aspirations of all laboring men. This has been more true in the South than in the North, but at various times in our history it has been applicable to all parts of the country.

Along with this, industry has long been guilty of stereotyping in job classifications. Only the menial jobs—the hot, heavy and hard—were available to Negroes. At times this has also applied to other minorities, usually the foreign-born; but there has been a difference. The way to advancement was blocked only temporarily for those minorities whose skins were white. Eager to get a toe-hold when they first arrived here, the Irish were once pushed easily into this classification. This is no longer true, while it has actually taken a war to bring about the upgrading of Negroes. And even with this advance the percentage of Negro workers who have risen to the status of foreman is pathetically small.

15

# THE HIGH COST OF PREJUDICE

Industry has justified this position by borrowing from the same legend which the South has so effectively utilized. Yet the assumption that Negroes cannot master anything but unskilled work is borne out neither in practice nor in history. The South's picture of a slave class which was only capable of unskilled work seems logical so long as we think only in terms of cotton culture. But we were not the industrial nation then that we are today; and the plantation was nearly self-sufficient, because everything had to be produced on the home place save that which was sent in at high prices. As a result an artisan class was necessary, and in the South it was for the most part made up of Negroes with a heritage of skilled labor dating back to the seventeenth century.

Before cotton became the staple crop of the South, tobacco was the main moneymaker. Planters depended on the skill, as well as the brawn, of Negro laborers. Slave carpenters, coopers, blacksmiths, dyers, tanners, bricklayers and shoemakers were common on the plantations of the tobacco belt as early as the last half of the seventeenth century. Most of the buildings in the South, up to the time of the Civil War, were the work of Negro carpenters, and eventually, when the production of iron and clothing was instituted commercially, it was Negro labor which was widely utilized.

Why, then, with this background, should the Negro eventually have found himself relegated to an unskilled status? The answer is that it happened with purpose in the South and more or less haphazardly in the North. Toward the end of the Civil War the outward status of the slave suddenly changed. Where he had once been able to work for hire only if he were a free Negro or, in a limited sense, when he was put out for hire by his master and allowed to keep a fraction of his earning power to be applied toward purchasing his freedom, he now depended entirely on wages. At the same time, the skilled jobs he had been performing became desirable to others, namely the poor whites who had been trying unsuccessfully to wrest a living from the soil.

The consequent usurpation of most skilled jobs by whites has been more or less gradual, but it has also been complete. In the construction field, where the Negro had his strongest hold, it has been perhaps most gradual; but new building methods and materials, the freezing out of Negroes by the craft unions of the AFofL (or at best the use of separate but powerless jim crow unions) have all done their work well. There are still Negroes in the construction trades in the South, but there has been a great drop in their number. In heavy industry the Negro was quickly pushed back into menial work, where he worked longer and harder for lower wages. In textiles and tobacco, where the Negro has managed to hold onto some skilled jobs, again we find that they are the least desirable ones. Often these are outside jobs, or jobs based on a wage differential. Some are even based on a production schedule so high that normally it is impossible to earn decent wages. Barbering and catering, once predominantly Negro, are now monopolized by whites. Even the Negro bell boy has been squeezed out in some areas of the South, a result of the last depression.

In the North it was assumed that the South, having the largest percentage of colored population, knew most about

17

how to deal with it, and the same pattern emerged in many areas. It differed in quality, but it was nonetheless a part of the industrial picture.

On first look it would seem that industry benefited by such a policy. Labor costs are usually the largest item in any manufacturing process. If they are kept low through discriminatory employment practices, profits should be that much higher. Yet this is only partially true, for real profits lie in mass production, since the more one produces the lower the unit cost is likely to be. Such profits are not forthcoming, however, if there is not enough purchasing power in the community, or the nation, to buy most of the goods produced. We found this out in the last depression, and even in normal years there is apt to be a surplus which we try to take up by such methods as installment buying, not always a satisfactory method by any manner of means.

There are two schools of thought on the relationship between production and purchasing power. One claims that the lower the production cost the higher will be the purchasing power, that if we produce enough cheaply enough everyone will be able to buy even with low wages. There are others who maintain that if we keep our purchasing power up through high wages we will be able to buy enough to keep production at a point where industry will profit. But either way, so long as the purchasing power of the Negro is limited by discrimination, you immediately limit at least one potential customer out of ten, which hardly seems good business.

Another side to this is the effect on the community. For

example, a number of communities have offered special inducements to industry to move into their area, usually a low purchase price for a factory site, with payment spread out over a number of years and tax exemptions all along the line. Certainly there is no sense in saying that a community does not benefit when a large industry moves in. A new pay roll affects any area: workers spend more money in local stores, buy homes or other property and contribute to local tax revenue. But the point is that if a community offers too many inducements and the incoming industrial unit pays very low wages, partially due to prejudice or discrimination, the benefits are much lower than they might otherwise be.

One of the most costly luxuries for any community is a ghetto, whether it be racial or merely low-income. The strain that an industrial influx makes upon the existing facilities usually means expanded social services. School needs become greater, and, if the workers who make this extension necessary do not share adequately in the additional tax burden, the benefit to the community from the new industry may hardly be worth the increased budget. If on the other hand such an industry brings into the community a pay roll that is adequately distributed regardless of race, creed or color, the benefits to everyone are obvious.

This way of looking at the cost of prejudice may not seem applicable now that we are in a period of prosperity. But it is applicable in normal times; and in periods of depression it is particularly so, since it is always the minority groups who suffer most and consequently place the heaviest burdens on social services and relief needs.

19

# THE HIGH COST OF PREJUDICE

And let us not overlook the fact that prejudice and discrimination in our industrial war effort very nearly cost us victory. At the outbreak of the war abroad we were not geared industrially to be the production center of the world and few of us realized the bigness of the task before us. Those were the days when our newly drafted soldiers were training with wooden guns and stove pipe anti-aircraft artillery—when we had almost no air force and not enough ships to take care of even our own needs.

Soon it became apparent that it was up to industry to convert to a wartime basis as rapidly as possible and, after Pearl Harbor, to prepare for any eventuality. The main eventuality was a manpower shortage. At the rate that the armed services were taking young men, it was plain that the bottom of the manpower barrel would soon be in sight. The women who were in those days going into industry could only postpone the crisis for a short time. Yet in the face of all this what was the position of the Negro? The truth is that in a period when industry was crying for workers and unable to get enough to maintain production schedules, there was wide unemployment among Negroes!

This was particularly true in aircraft, where as late as September, 1941, a survey by the Bureau of Employment Security showed that only 5.9 per cent of the companies employed Negroes; 24.3 per cent did not then employ Negroes although they expressed a willingness to do so in the future, and 69.8 per cent of the firms did not then, and did not intend to, employ Negroes in the future. Nor was the picture in most other industries much brighter. Everywhere was the same paradox—newspaper ads pleading for war workers, while a tenth of the available labor supply was excluded from many war jobs.

Government was aware of this. The Negro was considered, if not included, from the very inception of the war effort. Certain agencies, and even the Congress, had made ambiguous statements urging that there be no discrimination on account of race, creed or color, but management for the most part had ignored the hints. The National Defense Advisory Commission discussed with labor unions the problem of getting Negroes into the war effort, but with at least one union there remained the problem of union discrimination. After a shaky start federal vocational training was being given to Negroes, but what was the value in this when the Negro found it virtually impossible to get a job after completing his training course?

Negroes, quite rightly, were bitter, and when their protests were ignored they decided to take direct action. A. Philip Randolph, head of the Brotherhood of Sleeping Car Porters, organized the March on Washington Movement, a demonstration by fifty thousand colored men and women, from all parts of the country, who planned to dramatize their plight by a march down Pennsylvania Avenue in Washington. Fearful of public reaction, the Administration attempted to have the demonstration called off, but the leaders remained firm. Words were no longer enough, they said; either machinery must be set up for direct action or the march would take place as scheduled.

Executive Order 8802 was the result, issued by the President on June 25, 1941. It put into concrete words the hitherto ambiguous policy of nondiscrimination in all government war work. It was also the basis of the Fair

Employment Practices Commission, which all minority groups recently attempted to make a permanent agency, only to have it filibustered to death by a handful of Southern Senators.

There are those who claim that FEPC was not necessary, then or at the present time. One might agree that it would not seem necessary in a democracy, yet a look at the facts proves otherwise. Four months after the Presidential order was issued, a hearing was held in Los Angeles to determine how well the aircraft factories were carrying out the policy contained in 8802. It was found that one large company employed 33,000 workers and only ten of them were Negroes. In another, which employed 48,000, fifty-five Negroes had recently been hired under threat of the hearing. In a third there were eight Negroes on the pay roll, and all of them were janitors. Hearings elsewhere turned up much the same statistics and met with little opposition save in the South, where it was claimed that FEPC was a plot instigated by the Communists in order to bring about social equality overnight.

Perhaps FEPC was not perfect, but certainly it helped break the back of the manpower shortage. Yet in every instance where it came up, either for renewal of funds or permanent status, Southern reactionaries fought it with relentless fury. Some firms resisted in spite of FEPC, though this was not always the fault of management. Unions which discriminated against Negroes, either by actual exclusion or by means of segregated and powerless auxiliary unions, likewise did their share. Workers themselves, as in the case of an Atlanta shirtmaker who was nearly forced to close his plant because his white workers refused to work in the same room with Negroes, also contributed. But in many cases a realistic policy by management would have held such incidents to a minimum.

The war is over now, and we are in the midst of reconversion. In most instances industry still needs the Negro worker, though there have been cases where Negroes have already been laid off and replaced by white workers.

It would not seem to the advantage of management to return to the old patterns. Negroes have learned the value of standing together with white workers and they are not likely to forget that lesson. One of the largest unions is bound to a policy of resisting discrimination, and even if there is a surplus of white workers available it seems unlikely that they will go back on their present policy. There is no doubt that the Negro brought a great impetus to the spread of that union and its administration is well aware of the fact.

Nor can management fall back on the old excuses. Skilled labor by Negroes proved itself in this war period, and surveys show that the once claimed black mark of absenteeism is no more applicable to black workers than to white. And in the South, where new workers had to be trained from scratch, it was found that there is little or no difference in the aptitudes of Negroes and whites. In fact in some instances it was discovered that Negroes learned faster since they had more incentive.

Social pressures are likely to remain firm against the integration of Negroes into industry on anything resembling an equal basis with whites. This does not mean, however, that management cannot bring about a modification of

23

that policy, or at least make certain that the gains already made are not lost. The difference between a realistic policy and one which is weak and unrealistic has been shown in numerous racial incidents. Where an equitable racial employment policy was of long standing, or even if new was firmly applied, there were few instances of work stoppages over the upgrading of colored workers. On the other hand where white workers knew that management had no policy and was unlikely to take a firm stand, such stoppages did occur. Two good examples are the sitdown strikes which occurred at Wright Aeronautical and Packard.

Such racial demonstrations were nothing short of criminal in wartime. In peacetime the least that one can say is that they are equally costly to management and the community. If management hopes, however, that through such strife will come a general weakening of labor, that is another thing altogether. The chances that union busting may be effected by a split in the CIO over the race issue seem very doubtful indeed. In fact the suspicion is that such action would be more likely to strengthen the CIO. As to the AFofL, particularly in the South, there is some chance of success; but not on a national scale. All in all it is hard to see what management could hope to gain by such a policy.

Not to be forgotten, of course, is the ticklish question of union seniority, which will work real hardship on Negro workers in some instances. In some industries where the Negro has a record of skilled work of long standing he will be able to hold his own. But in others, for example aircraft where he was not employed before 1941–42, he has little hope of keeping his foot in the door. Even with a majority of women giving up their war jobs, the Negro's outlook in regard to union seniority is far from bright.

It seems likely, however, that some compromises on seniority may be made in those instances where hardship is most severe, if so doing will not weaken the basic structure of the union. Both management and labor have a great deal to lose if there is not more participation by Negroes. If both are sincere, the chances are we will see more and more integration as the years pass. For one thing the Negro is in perhaps the best position of any minority to exert pressures, if he starts losing out in the employment picture. His vote is a pivotal one in the North, where industrialization is heaviest. Thrown either way it is likely to be a decisive factor in a close election. Both parties know this and both parties need the Negro vote. The CIO knows that the Negro is far too important a cog in the wheel of all progressive action to take a chance on forcing him into the camp of the opposition. Judging by the past record, the AFofL is less likely to put up a fight for the Negro worker, but even here it is difficult to make any certain prognostications.

## CHAPTER THREE

## UNIONS WITHIN UNIONS

THE ATTITUDES which unions show toward Negroes varies all the way from complete exclusion to full acceptance. There is also, in many instances, a wide variance between the stated policy and how it is actually carried out, between national unions and their many affiliates, and even among the various locals themselves. And on the whole, craft unions are much more likely to discriminate against Negroes than are industrial unions.

Before looking into the results of such discriminations let us go back a little into the history of unions and their relationships with Negroes. The Negro was first introduced into northern industry on a large scale as a strikebreaker, which can be traced partially to the exclusiveness of the unions themselves. Few Negroes had a chance to belong to unions and as a result had little education along trades union lines. Management went into the deep South for these new recruits and naturally did not bother to inform such workers of the rôle they were expected to play. It seems doubtful that Negroes had any conception why so many white workers hated them, assuming the reasons to be purely racial. Once they did understand, however, we have examples of their refusing to act as scabs. One of the most dramatic occurred in the Latrobe Steel and Coupler strike of 1901.

# UNIONS WITHIN UNIONS

In order to help break the strike the company had brought in by train three hundred Negroes from Alabama. The coaches in which they came were left on a deserted spur some distance from the plant, which was located in a Chicago suburb. Four white men from the Chicago Federation of Labor learned of this maneuver and managed to contact the Negro workers and explain the real issues at stake. The result was that the newcomers refused to act as strikebreakers and were sent back to Alabama, a factor which was instrumental in the winning of the strike by the union.

Such incidents are perhaps isolated examples, but they did occur. Yet the more usual thing was for unions not to bother to go to the trouble of explaining the basic issues. As a result white workers were resentful toward Negro workers, especially in their rôle of strikebreaker; and Negroes were equally resentful toward whites because of their enmity. There is little doubt that management used this schism for its own ends; and it is interesting that in several cases where the unions had interracial solidarity, such a policy had little effect. It did not work with the United Mine Workers of America, which from its inception in 1890 refused to bar Negroes. Of course most strikebreakers lost their jobs once the strike was broken, but those few Negroes who had been able to join unions learned the value of a common stand by *all* working men and stayed on to form a small but potent nucleus of interracial and working-class solidarity which was of great value to unions.

The largest influx of Negroes into industry came during the first World War. When immigration was cut off from

27

Europe, the pinch in industrial manpower was felt almost immediately, and thousands of Negroes migrated North in search of better jobs. Some came of their own volition, drawn by the magnet of high wages, but by far the greatest number were recruited by labor agents sent South by industry. Not all remained after the war was over and a depression spread over the land; many were laid off, and those who were not found themselves faced with shrinking wages or less desirable jobs. But the point is that they had their foot in the door and they meant to keep it there. The thought of returning to the less liberal racial mores of the South helped to make up for the suffering which many Negroes in this period were forced to undergo. And those who could joined unions, some through closed-shop agreements but the majority because they wanted the added strength of union membership.

The craft unions of the American Federation of Labor were in control and, though they had no set policy against Negro membership, certain subterfuges were commonly employed to keep Negroes out. One of these was the auxiliary union, the union within a union, whereby the AFofL was able to benefit from the Negro as a member, yet give him few of the benefits which membership usually brought.

At the inception of the American Federation of Labor each candidate for affiliation had been forced to pledge "never to discriminate against a fellow-worker on account of color, creed or nationality." But these fine words did not remain long in effect. Seeing a chance for rapid development, the AFofL evolved a policy of not letting its right hand know what its left was doing. It has remained in that never-never land down to the present day. Such a course has been broad enough to hold loosely together an organization of unions some of which do not bar Negroes and others which either do bar them or limit membership to separate unions for colored members.

Most craft unions had originated as fraternal or benevolent societies, and the idea of Negro membership, particularly in the South, seemed too closely akin to the dreaded social equality. It was also true that few Negroes, up to the large-scale migrations to the industrial North, were in industry. Outside of the construction trades the Southern Negro was mainly rural, and his exclusion offered no real threat to the initial expansion of the union.

At a later date, when social pressures developed and Negro workers increased numerically, the auxiliary union looked like the perfect compromise. At first segregated unions within unions seemed to satisfy everyone, even the Negro. But paying dues and getting nothing in return, having no say in union affairs and, most of all, the bitter realization that white union members were getting better wages and working conditions, made Negroes wake up in a hurry. They have been yelling ever since, but to little avail.

At every AFofL convention the able A. Philip Randolph of the Brotherhood of Sleeping Car Porters has brought to the floor the question of union discrimination. Each time he and the small block who supported him have been ruled out of order on technicalities, offered white-washed reports, or had their motion tabled until the next annual meeting.

# THE HIGH COST OF PREJUDICE

Individual unions of the AFofL have often been solidly behind the Negro in his struggle upward industrially, particularly in these war years; and some unions which discriminate in certain areas because of southern mores, do not do so elsewhere. But the overall policy and the leaders who formulate that policy seem determined to follow a middle-of-the-road policy of such elasticity that no stand will be necessary. Saying on one hand that there is nothing in the by-laws to exclude Negroes and that no union constitution may contain a clause excluding them, on the other hand they openly wink at the chicanery of initiation rituals, which include an oath that no member will introduce into the union any except "competent white men." The answer that a constitution is the affair of the AFofL, a ritual the business of the local, and to interfere would be a violation of the autonomy of an affiliate, is most certainly doubletalk.

So far the AFofL has managed to please more members than it has alienated. In its position as the "Aristocracy of Labor" it seems fairly secure, but one wonders for how long. There seems more than a faint suspicion that by trying to please everyone its leadership may eventually end up by pleasing no one.

From its very beginnings in 1935, the Congress of Industrial Organizations differed from the AFofL in two important respects. The AFofL, composed for the most part of craft unions, maintained its position by exercising control over a few highly skilled and strategically situated jobs, while the CIO planned to maintain bargaining power by opening its ranks to all the workers in a plant or industry.

Moreover, when the CIO talked about no discrimination it actually seemed to mean it.

The ramifications of this difference were widespread. For one thing it was a very efficient spike driven into management's old game of dividing white and Negro workers in order to weaken the union. In addition it opened up a whole new potential for union membership and it was not content to let the matter rest there. Although in the beginning Negro workers were not the important factor they were to become with the manpower shortage, the CIO took pains from the start to educate Negro workers, along with white workers, in the ways of trade unionism. Moreover, an anti-discrimination division was set up and an educational drive concerning minority rights was planned. A number of pamphlets and placards were issued so that when Negroes began to compete for better jobs a foundation had been laid and there was a stockpile of ammunition to use not only against management but also against prejudiced white workers.

Although it would be nice to say that there was no racial friction this would not be altogether true. Our mores run as deeply through the working class as through any other segment of our society. In the South there was the old problem of how to function without running into the familiar bugaboo of social equality, while at the same time making certain that Negro members had a full say in the doings of the local to which they belonged. A compromise was made to the extent that though Negroes served alongside whites on executive boards, white members sat on one side of the hall at meetings, Negroes on the other. It is true that this was a kind of segregation, but it was not the usual kind. And although not all locals followed out these instructions to the letter, the important thing is that the national policy was continually prodding them to fall into line.

Likewise there were instances where rank-and-file members tried to go against this policy and even resorted to wild-cat strikes on purely racial grounds. A case in point was the sitdown strike of CIO personnel in the Chrysler Highland Park Plant over the upgrading and transferring of qualified Negro workers. But a firm stand by union leaders and the officials of the plant showed that the CIO meant business. Like incidents at Packard and Wright again showed a firmness on the union's part. Once the rank and file learned that the union administration meant what it said and would not back down, such racial incidents ceased.

There is no doubt that this helped morale all along the line. Negroes more and more realized the benefits of a union card and brought a new spirit to the union. Some whites still grumbled a little, but most were relieved to get back to the serious business of producing to win a war. The production figures which resulted speak for themselves.

Another difference between the AFofL and CIO is their different reaction to the field of politics. The CIO, feeling that it was important to have candidates in office who would back progressive legislation, organized the Political Action Committee and its offshoot the National Citizens Political Action Committee. The AFofL, on the other hand, decided to leave campaigning strictly alone and function on the old level of horse trading.

## UNIONS WITHIN UNIONS

Our concern here is not with the rightness or wrongness of unions' entering politics—nor, in fact, even with the success of such ventures. What does interest us is how its nondiscrimination policy of the CIO aided the initial drive of NCPAC. The nature of the Negro vote in many areas locally and its overall strategic position nationally gave PAC a tremendous advantage. And PAC was able to count on that vote to a large degree because Negroes were some of the hardest workers in that movement.

As already stated the impulse which the Negro has brought to CIO all along the line has been tremendous. But in the light of post-war lay-offs, or possible depressions, what will be the effect of discrimination, or the lack of it, on the two big unions?

At the moment it seems unlikely that either the AFofL or the CIO will radically change its policies through internal action. Negroes in the CIO are here to stay, though it has been estimated that union seniority could cost Negro workers sixty to ninety per cent of their jobs. But it seems doubtful that the CIO will let anything like these figures be realized, and a better guess seems that somewhere along the line there may be a compromise, possibly where the worst hardships exist. On past record it seems unlikely that the AFofL will be willing to make any compromise. In fact the suspicion is that the higher the figure the happier union officials will be, in spite of the fact that some affiliates have lowered the color bar and now admit Negroes freely.

There is another factor to be considered, however, namely the increased pressures which may be brought to bear against discrimination in unions. The legal department of the National Association for the Advancement of Colored People was quick to see the relationship between union discrimination and Executive Order 8802, the Fair Employment Practices Commission, and the various state anti-bias laws. When they took the matter into the courts action was not long in coming. The Supreme Court of the United States, in a suit brought by Negro railroad workers against the Railway Brotherhoods, ruled that unions certified by the National Mediation Board have the positive duty to represent *all* workers within a craft without discrimination. The Supreme Court of California, in a similar suit against the Boilermakers Union, has also ruled that a union which has won, or desires to win, a closed-shop agreement must admit Negroes to membership on the same terms and conditions applicable to non-Negroes.

In each case an AFofL union was the guilty party; moreover, other AFofL unions continue to disobey and circumvent such rulings whenever and wherever possible. This is bad publicity for unions, never too popular in the public eye; but it is also potentially dangerous to the whole labor movement.

No one knows the eventual outcome, but one of three things seems likely to happen. John L. Lewis, with a long record of non-bias from the old United Mine Worker days, seems slated for leadership in the AFofL he recently rejoined. Personally ambitious and bitter toward his old friends in the CIO, it is possible that he will tend to modify racial discrimination, if only to increase his own following. Such action on his part might be smart politics.

But if such internal action on the part of the AFofL is

not shortly forthcoming, the government may be forced to step in. Public pressure may make it necessary. If this does not force the AFofL to cease its discriminatory practices, federal control seems inevitable. The result would be a great loss in prestige with the public, not only for the AFofL but for the whole trades-union movement. It is probable that if this happened union membership would fall off rapidly for obvious reasons.

The third possibility is that the CIO and the AFofL will fight it out on racial grounds. If the CIO were successful the AFofL might be relegated to its original position, simply a loosely jointed combination of fraternal and benevolent societies without real power or importance. In fact the first stages of that battle are being fought right now in the South where the CIO is making a strong drive for increased membership and is being fought by the AFofL with all the racial hysteria and bigotry such organizations as the Klan have utilized. The outcome remains to be seen, but one thing is clear. The racial issues in the campaign are hurting the whole labor movement, which is another example of how costly prejudice and discrimination are to those who practice them.

## CHAPTER FOUR

## WOULD YOU LET YOUR OWN CONTRACTOR
## GET AWAY WITH IT?

SOMEWHERE IN a large Northern city there is a land-lord who thinks he is getting rich. He owns an apartment house in what was formerly an all-white neighborhood, but when the near-by black ghetto burst its seams and spilled over into the area, his white tenants moved out. He had always heard that whenever Negroes moved into a residential neighborhood real estate values went down, but now he has found a way to actually increase his financial return.

It was really a very simple operation. His building was largely made up of six-room units, apartments which he had rented to white tenants for sixty dollars a month. Now he merely turned all of the rooms into kitchenettes, one-room units which he rented for eight dollars a week. Where his return had once been only sixty dollars on each six-room unit it is now one hundred and ninety-two dollars. Not only that: because his new tenants are colored and hemmed in from moving elsewhere because of prejudice and discrimination, he has also found it possible to cut operating expenses to almost nothing by doing little or no repair work, painting or other services.

In this case it looks as though prejudice were making our landlord rich, but actually there are indirect costs which affect the whole city and hidden costs which affect him as well. By such tactics he has created, or helped to create, the following situation. His area has the highest tubercular rate in the city—the greatest incidence of crime and prostitution, more venereal disease, the highest maternal-infant mortality figures, a higher insanity curve and, in hard times, a relief load which is staggering. Moreover, by his own actions he has done more to lower the value of his property than his Negro tenants ever did.

If this seems overdrawn the results of a recent survey in New York's Harlem prove otherwise. One day the city inspectors made a tour of the block bounded by West 118th and 117th Streets on the north and south, and Fifth and Lenox on the east and west. The National Urban League, an interracial group interested in housing conditions, had suggested the survey. In all, sixty-four buildings were visited, containing a total of seven hundred and sixteen apartments. In every instance violations of the building code were discovered, ranging all the way from gaping holes in ceilings and walls to broken staircases. Garbage and trash were piled high in the back yards, and most of the buildings were infested with rats.

Another case in point is Atlanta, Georgia, where in 1941 slum areas, predominantly segregated, paid only 5½% of the city's real property tax revenue and cost the city 53% of its police, fire, health and other service costs. In San Francisco 20% of the city's area contains 33% of the population, 60% of the t. b., 55% of the juvenile delinquency, 50% of the arrests, 45% of the city service costs, 35% of fires, yet brings in only 6% of the tax revenues. Again, in Spring-field, Illinois, it costs $3,200,000 a square mile to maintain slums which only contribute $586,000 in tax collections.

# THE HIGH COST OF PREJUDICE

Those who claim that such conditions are common to all slums and that we will always have slums, are in reality robbing their own pockets. Social services are becoming more and more costly and actually less and less able to stem the tide of crime and disease. Nor is there likely to be a turn for the better until some radical changes are made. Slums are like boilers that have too much steam up, and in the case of the black ghetto there is no escape valve.

Anyone who has read Richard Wright's *Native Son* has probably come as near to an approximation of what it is like to live in a racial ghetto as possible, but without actually living there no one can really know. A black ghetto differs from an ordinary slum in one important respect. In the ordinary slum it is possible, when one's financial conditions reach a certain point, to move out into other residential districts in the city. With the Negro it is almost universally true that he will be kept within the segregated areas. Restrictive covenants or public pressures will see to that.

The restrictive covenant is the main weapon used in keeping up the walls of the black ghetto. In simple terms it is an agreement between all the property owners in a given district that none of the signers will rent or sell their property to Negroes, the usual wording being "those not of the Caucasian race." Often it is also used to apply to Jews, but the Negro is always the main victim.

From a legal standpoint restrictive covenants have been acknowledged as lawful in some instances and as invalid in others. The Supreme Court has never ruled on one, though several state supreme courts have. Where one has been broken it has usually been through a ruling that, since some Negroes had been in the neighborhood before the covenant was made, it could not be held binding.

Our main interest in restrictive covenants, however, is in relationship to the prejudices which were responsible for their origin. Let us look for a moment at the attitudes of whites toward Negroes as neighbors. There is no doubt that this attitude is negative, but the interesting thing is that segregation has made it practically impossible for whites to really know what kind of neighbors Negroes might make. They have never had the experience of living alongside a colored family. Their reaction, then, is based purely on the folklore level.

If whites are so strongly opposed, why are restrictive covenants broken? The answer is that segregated areas are virtually never static, but rather extend and expand to a point where something must give, and then burst out at the seams. Whites living near-by under the supposed protection of a restrictive covenant eventually find themselves a white island in the midst of a black sea. Before long, one property owner, who has always been warned that his property would be deflated under such conditions, finds instead that he can actually sell at a good profit. Or an apartment-house owner finds that he can rent his apartments to Negroes for twenty-five, or even fifty per cent higher than his white tenants are willing to pay. The picture has suddenly radically changed yet neither is able to take advantage of the change. Both must sell or rent only to whites who will not pay such prices, or break their word on the covenant. In other words prejudice is costing them money. Very often they sell; and, once this happens and more than a handful of Negroes come into the neighborhood, there is an exodus of whites.

There is, of course, another alternative, that of remaining in the neighborhood; but few whites have the courage to do so. They may tarry long enough to find out that a few Negroes make good neighbors. Yet before long their prejudices, which originally created black ghettoes, have subjected them to higher food prices, less public services and so on. In other words they suffer, along with their Negro neighbors, all the disadvantages of segregated life.

This exact situation happens often enough to show all the elements of a vicious cycle. Race prejudice, residential segregation and economic interests all mutually reinforce one another. A few Negro families move in, and a few white families move out in protest. Because the black ghetto is always bursting at the seams from overcrowding, more Negroes follow. Then white residents, fearing the neighborhood will soon be all Negro, move out in a body, their prejudices reinforced. But actually if there were no segregation the circle might never be completed.

As a matter of fact, in certain isolated areas, when Negroes have moved in the majority of whites have remained, soon learning to respect their new neighbors; and, though close social ties do not usually develop, there is often very little racial tension. Negroes are so glad to get out of the ghetto that they are even more interested in keeping up their property than are white residents in the same area. After whites have a chance to get used to the idea it makes sense; it is better to have a good neighbor who happens to be colored than a poor one who is white.

# WOULD YOU LET YOUR OWN CONTRACTOR?

Until we can break down the black ghetto into an ordinary slum which can be dealt with on economic lines, we can make little progress. At present the pressures which segregated racial areas exert, especially at those points where the pressure is strong enough to bend the walls, form one of the main causes of racial tensions. These tensions are the stuff of which riots are made. They are the festering sores which break out into the gang warfare of frustrated adolescents. They are the breeding grounds which racists and bigots exploit.

But such areas affect us in yet another way. They and the prejudiced thinking which cause them have a great influence on our government in many ways, for example, public housing and city planning. We have definite proof that better housing facilities are one of the few constructive remedies for slums in general and racial slums in particular. By themselves they are far from a magical cure, but they are a big step in the right direction. Yet in the war years, when federal housing was limited to the construction of temporary quarters for war workers, much of the ground already gained was lost. One result is that segregated areas have swollen almost beyond recognition due to the influx of Negroes into industrial areas.

As soon as possible we will have to engage in vast new housing projects—some financed by public funds, others by private investors on the pattern set by some of the larger insurance companies in the past few years. The main problem posed is whether they shall be segregated or open to qualified people regardless of race, creed or color. This is more difficult of solution than it may at first appear and certainly it makes the job of city planning more difficult than it might overwise be. Politicians have an easier time of it. They find out what the majority of the voters want, vote through the funds, and then let the planners (city, state or federal), try to figure out a way to get out of the muddle which our prejudices have created.

Here are some of the difficulties. If your city has a large Negro population, as most large cities do, the greatest need for public, or semi-public housing will be found there. If you live in the South, token Negro housing projects will be built, under full segregation. But if you live in the North, though pressures for segregation may be as strong, other elements will enter the picture. Those who do not want such projects segregated will offer just as logical arguments for their point of view.

Actually those who have studied city planning pretty much agree that the most practical and economic plan, from the long term view, is a non-segregated project located where it can drain off some of the overcrowded black ghetto and eventually help to eliminate the patterns which created such ghettoes in the first place. Yet the short term view cannot be ignored either. People in ghettoes are desperately in need of housing too. But the whole trouble with segregated housing, even if equal or superior to that provided for whites, is that it merely perpetuates the same old problems.

There is, of course, no concrete blueprint to fit all situations. Before the war, for example, there were segregated Negro projects near white areas where the rents were too high to keep them fully occupied by Negroes. A financial loss resulted which would not have occurred had whites been able to live there too. Again there were some projects for whites only partially rented because they were located in areas where there was not enough demand for complete occupancy. Had there been no segregation policy in both instances this loss in revenue could have been avoided.

Basically, however, the nub of the whole problem is simply the fact that the unmeasurable cost of racial ghettoes (and it is increasing with the years) is slowly driving us into bankruptcy. Furthermore the racial tensions which segregation perpetuates, constitute a real threat to us all, black and white alike. In some areas we have seen this threat erupt into violence. Detroit is one good example, and the conditions really responsible for that ugliness have in no sense been eliminated. Until they are, we can, and probably will, have similar violence. Nor is the steam which escaped in Detroit any guarantee that outbreaks may not occur elsewhere. Race riots unfortunately are a recurring disease, and vaccination, not patent medicine, is what is most needed.

That Negroes and whites can live together has been amply demonstrated. One of the best examples started out with all of the racial tensions which we have been led to believe rule out such experiments; but, once the whites involved learned that those in authority meant to stick by their guns, things were rapidly ironed out.

The Sojourner Truth Housing Project, a federal housing unit for war workers in Detroit, was completed early in 1942. Located in a predominantly white neighborhood, there was a great deal of agitation against its being opened to Negro tenants, as had been originally planned. Pressure was brought to bear upon the government authorities to have the project turned over to whites, and such an order was actually sent to˙ Detroit, after two * white Federal Housing officials resigned in protest. But Detroit Negroes filed a restraining order, and when they picketed the city hall, Mayor Edward Jeffries as quickly asked the federal authorities to reverse themselves, which they did. By this time a year had passed, a year when there was a great need for housing in Detroit and the lack of it had direct bearing on war production.

When the original policy was again established, whites threatened to resist by force if Negroes moved in. The opening date was postponed again, in the hope that an amicable settlement could be worked out. About the middle of February a delegation of Negroes went to Washington, and after consultation with Federal Housing authorities February 23 was announced as the day when the project would be formally opened.

On the night of February 22 there was a large demonstration at which a fiery cross was burned, the symbol of the supposedly defunct Ku Klux Klan, a rather clear indication that all the pressure was not coming from the residents of the neighborhood. When the new tenants arrived on the following day with moving vans, they were met by a mob estimated at approximately a thousand whites. A pitched battle took place in which twenty-five were seriously injured, in spite of an emergency squad of one hundred and fifty police, who arrived on the scene well after the trouble started.

---

* Clark Foreman and Nathan Straus, Jr.

---

# WOULD YOU LET YOUR OWN CONTRACTOR?

The project remained uninhabited, while white and Negro liberals held daily meetings urging the mayor to take action. Punitive measures had been of the usual pattern; most of those arrested had been Negroes who were in reality fighting to protect their own homes. On the 15th of April federal authorities instructed the local officials to proceed with the occupancy of the project. Two weeks later a thousand state troopers escorted the two hundred Negro families into their new homes and remained on guard until they were settled. Although a smaller patrol was maintained for a short time no further violence was reported, nor has there been any since.

The Sojourner Truth incident is interesting for several reasons. Although it was quasi-segregated in nature, its location in the midst of a white neighborhood broke the usual pattern slightly. There is very little doubt from the investigation afterward that much of the impetus for the violence was furnished by outside agitators. This is something not uncommon to mob violence in all areas, but Detroit, because of the great influx of Southern whites over a period of years, is in many ways a city Southern in nature. It is a hotbed of racist organizations of every description. The most important thing, however, is that, once local authorities showed they meant business, racial tensions were shattered to the extent that new patterns could be started without further incident.

Like incidents have been repeated elsewhere, sometimes with the same initial tensions, often without them. Typical is Marin City, an aggregation of fifteen hundred housing units located seven miles from San Francisco and adjacent to Oakland, hub of several large shipyards. The

45

project was built for shipyard workers, and its population of five thousand includes a thousand Negroes and more than a sprinkling of native-born Southern whites. A policy of non-segregation is well established.

When a Southerner moves in and finds a Negro family in his unit he usually goes to the management in horrified indignation, but all his threats and blustering accomplish is to have the manager tell him that if he is not satisfied with the arrangements he can move out, there are others waiting who do not feel that way. Most of them stay, for Marin City rents are reasonable and the surroundings pleasant.

Negroes and whites seem to mingle even at social functions without outward animosity. Man is a creature of habit and once he gets used to a new idea it loses much of its terror. As one white Texan put it in an interview which appeared in *Common Ground* magazine: "I don't like it at all. But we get along all right. We don't have much to do with them, of course. We say 'howdy' and my kids go to the same school with theirs. We don't have any trouble. There's no trouble between whites and Negroes at Marin City."

Incidents like this point to a better future, though the progress seems agonizingly slow. They point to a time when the black ghetto may become just another slum and can be dealt with accordingly. Unless this happens we are going to pay more and more for our prejudices, until we reach a point where we can no longer afford such foolishness.

## CHAPTER FIVE

# FROM BIGGER THOMAS TO LITTLE CAESAR

IT HAS been estimated that every time the clock ticks crime has cost us eleven dollars and fifty cents. If we could cut this figure by half, or even by a third, we would save ourselves money which could be spent to much greater advantage elsewhere. Prejudice and discrimination are not wholly responsible for making criminals, but for a moment just consider one fact. How many criminals do you read about in the daily papers who do not belong to a minority group?

Some people, of course, see in this the rash generalization that there must be a latent criminal streak in all minority groups. But this is dangerous reasoning, since science maintains that criminal tendencies are not a racial characteristic. Moreover the sociologist sees a close connection between crime and environment, and the case histories of most criminals point to a slum background.

Naturally it would be senseless to place the whole blame on prejudice and discrimination. Substandard living conditions affect the physical makeup of all kinds of individuals. But when the added stigma of inferiority is placed on an individual and his basic drive is shut off from normal outlets, a potential breeding ground for crime is the probable result. This is not to infer that any individual faced with such an environment will turn out a criminal, but merely that the odds are tipped in that direction. To put

47

it another way, society has made it more difficult for individuals from such an environment to fulfil their normal aspirations.

By normal aspirations is simply meant a chance to make a decent living, to maintain a certain status in the community and society at large, and to marry and raise a family, knowing that one's children will have an opportunity to better themselves. If this is denied through ordinary channels, other outlets will be developed and utilized by at least a part of those discriminated against. The Italian boy who might have been another Joe DiMaggio may turn out to be a gangster; the Greek who might have been a successful business man may grow up to be a gambler; the Negro who might have been a CPA may end up in the numbers racket.

There are, of course, other factors to be considered. Home life, particularly where the mother does not have to work in order to keep the family going, is of great importance. The national customs of some of the foreign born seek to hold down competition in things American to a minimum, something else which may counterbalance the scales. Yet it is interesting to note that usually the second or third generation is eager to be caught up in the search for the American dream. Sooner or later the youngsters strive for status on American terms.

Not to be ignored either is the unvarnished truth that as a nation we glamorize the successful criminal. The gangster has been given a certain standing in our literature and, in particular, our motion pictures. The racketeer is often recognized as a big shot, almost on a par with the banker or the successful industrialist. The effect which this has on underprivileged youngsters, especially those suffering from an inferiority stigma, is not hard to imagine. Such figures become, in a sense, racial heroes and it is not difficult to understand why.

But of all the minority groups the Negro shows most clearly the relationship between crime and our prejudices and discriminations. There has been a great deal of nonsense written and handed down by word of mouth and much of it has been conflicting. As a result the waters are muddied rather than clarified. Negroes who commit crimes are almost universally identified by race in newspaper accounts. Even in the North a Negro crime story rates the front page, while comparable crimes committed by other racial elements are usually relegated to the middle of the paper. That crime is an element in Negro life, just as it is in the life of all peoples, no thinking person will deny. But all too frequently it is blown up out of all proportion to its relative importance.

One factor which is all too frequently overlooked is the prevalent attitude of the Southern community toward crime and the Negro. It is important not only in the South but nationally, for Southern racial mores have been, until recent years, the basis of all our racial thinking. This Southern attitude is many-faceted and sometimes so complex that it rivals the old gag about which comes first, the chicken or the egg. Yet not to attempt an understanding of its implications makes any clarification of the whole picture nigh unto impossible.

At the bottom is to be found the old story of segregation—of the separation of the races, of dual public facilities, of a clearly defined wage differential, and actually of two sets of personal responsibilities. An example of this is to be found in the relationship which normally exists between employer and domestic servant in the South. Today, with industry having cut domestic service to a minimum and raised wages accordingly, it is less true than it has been in the past. But basically the following is fairly typical.

Normally the domestic wages of a Negro house worker in the South will vary between three and ten dollars for a full week's work with two afternoons off. It may be higher in certain areas but in others it has been even lower. The work is hard and usually limited to one house worker. As a result it has become a more or less accepted part of the regional mores that, as a compensation for low wages and hard work, a servant has a right to carry home leftovers. Leftovers, never clearly defined, could mean a great many things, usually whatever a servant was able to get away with. Unless it reached a point where things of real value disappeared, it was ignored by employer and employee alike.

This was not limited to any part of the South, and it has been going on for so long that it has actually become a part of the folkway pattern. Whites, believing that all Negroes stole, laughed it off as just another aspect of the white man's burden. Negroes, trying to make ends meet and equalize low wages—but perhaps more important, playing a game that had certain rules—did not consider it stealing. It was just the way things were. It was a part of the curious relationship inherent in a racial etiquette that was confusing but inevitable.

On another level there has always been the ever present danger that a Negro might more easily be framed for something he did not do than punished for something he had actually done. So long as a Negro stayed clear of riling up the white folks, he was free to do pretty much anything he was able to get away with.

The ramifications of such a policy were and continue to be widespread in the South. One thing it has meant is that Negroes are left largely without police protection from the normal crime found in any community. White police are not interested in what happens in the segregated Negro community, so long as it does not create a ruckus. Negroes have grown to hate and fear white police and distrust a court of law, because they realize that without the help of a white man they have no fair chance of getting justice. Not only are Negroes segregated but as a result crime is largely segregated as well.

The attitudes of white police towards Negroes in the South range all the way from complete brutality to a condescending patronage. Graft from Negro gambling and prostitution seems to many Negroes the only interest white police have in the Negro community. Many sheriffs are not paid a straight salary in certain areas but are advanced so much for feeding each prisoner in the county or city jail. By cutting down on both the quality and the quantity of rations and keeping the jails full of Negroes, many a sheriff has retired a rich man. In some places, generally larger cities, experiments have been made with Negro police, and they have for the most part been successful. Yet this is not on a large enough scale to have any real significance save as a trend. All this, plus the lack of justice in the courts, has made most Negroes cynical about crime and with some justification.

But what most Negroes fear most is being framed for something in which they were not really involved. It is common to look for the nearest Negro when any crime has been committed, and this is especially true of sexual crimes, where any Negro near the scene stands a better than even chance of standing trial on a trumped up charge, or even undergoing the nightmare of mob violence.

Mentioned earlier is the important factor of a dual interpretation of punishment. Homicide among Negroes is a fairly minor offense, as is a white homicide against a Negro. But if a Negro kills a white man his punishment is final and absolute. Furthermore the penalty for sassing a white man is likely to be more severe than for killing another Negro. It makes a difference whom a Negro commits a crime *against,* and the difference goes all the way through the whole book of crimes.

Thus the mores of the South have created a pattern that makes any adequate law enforcement program nearly impossible to put into execution, and makes equally doubtful any clear picture of the Negro in relationship to crime from a statistical point of view. Negroes forced to live under such a pattern find themselves in a never-never world where too often they are unable to get a clear picture or even, seeing one, do anything constructive about it.

Coming North many Negroes have carried with them remnants of this same pattern, and this has in turn complicated the whole process of constructive law enforcement for Negroes as well as whites. For this reason crime prevention in Northern Negro communities is difficult for many of the same reasons that are found in the South, though to a lesser degree. The main difficulty is that wherever you set up a black ghetto you also segregate crime to the place where it is most likely to flourish, though not necessarily remain. Class structures in a Northern Negro community are well defined; but, so long as you throw everyone in together every which way, community social pressures are partially destroyed.

Negroes have also brought with them from the South a lasting hatred for white police, often with good reason. For even in the North many police have been guilty of brutality and rank discrimination in law enforcement. This was shown in Detroit where, although Negroes suffered most of the injuries and fatalities and whites were the aggressors, the majority of those arrested were Negroes. Nor is this an isolated case. It is no exaggeration to say that from bitter, personal experience the majority of Negroes, even in the North, look upon white police more as their enemies than their protectors. White police have for years shaken down Negro prostitutes and accepted bribes from Negro gambling interests. There is also the familiar feeling that white police are little interested in preventing crimes of Negroes against Negroes. Nor has the usual practice of sending white police into Negro precincts as punishment, done much to rectify this feeling.

This pattern of hatred and distrust is so deeply ingrained that, when police tend to treat Negroes fairly and without brutality—as under the LaGuardia administration in New York for example—it usually makes little difference. Negroes have seen police kick Negroes around for so long that they are never sure when a culprit, especially amongst youngsters, is a real criminal or another victim of the racial prejudice and discrimination that is a part of daily existence. For example the Harlem riot of 1935 exploded upon the rumor that a Negro boy, caught stealing a cheap knife in a five-and-ten-cent store, had been brutally beaten by the police. Our own prejudice has really created a situation where, even when we want to rectify our past errors, we have great trouble doing so.

Juvenile delinquency in the Negro community is a real problem. Nor can its increase be termed racial, since juvenile delinquency rates are up everywhere and in about the same proportions. But in the black ghetto it is more of a problem, because the pinch-penny policies our prejudices dictate have crippled those agencies best able to cope with it. Schools in most Negro communities are so overcrowded that in some areas they are actually functioning in three shifts, with a personnel inadequate to do more than teach the rudiments of the three R's. City social agencies are understaffed and unable to pay adequate salaries for assuring the kind of social workers best equipped to deal with the problem. Nor are there enough agencies to care for the children of parents, both of whom must work in order to maintain economic security. Kids who are forced to play in the streets pick up the ways of the street.

One offshoot of this is the Harlem gang, 'teen age kids banded together to rob, steal and mug their way into the newspaper headlines, or create the material for sensational articles in our national magazines. Here as well a great deal of nonsense has been written. Actually the counterpart of such gangs is to be found in any slum area; but what does make them infinitely more dangerous is the racial tensions which our prejudices have helped create. We have made life in the black ghetto so valueless, day to day existence so much harder, and the chance to break out so much more difficult, that such gangs are old beyond their years. They have been responsible for murder and sex crimes, and by no means all of their victims are white.

Usually the police are unable to do anything effective, for arrests seldom bring a sentence beyond the reform school level. Treating them rough brings the charge of police brutality, and police have not found the Negro community eager to help, since Negroes are never sure which may be a real criminal and which a neighborhood boy caught in a racial frameup. Also the community itself fears such gangs, because they are well organized and may retaliate against informers. They terrorize colored and white merchants alike, who pay them to leave their stores alone. Even Negro organizations are loath to step in, knowing that a real exposé, thanks to our prejudices, would bring about a general condemnation of all Negroes when only a small minority is at fault.

Social agencies are unable to do much about them either, because of a lack of funds and personnel. Private agencies want nothing to do with them. Such organizations as PAL, the Police Athletic League, do what they can, and public figures like Joe Louis and Canada Lee, who came up off the streets himself, work hard to show such kids that crime doesn't pay. But it's difficult work which only scratches the surface.

We have reached a point where it is apparent that the

55

policies we have been following just aren't doing the job. Nor will adding more police to the community or allowing the use of nightsticks to break up the outward manifestations, bring any sort of permanent solution. What is needed is something deeper and more basic.

This much seems certain: the cost of crime will more likely increase than decrease in the years to come. Unless we are willing to go on carrying that burden, we must understand the basic cause of that part of crime which can be traced to prejudice and discrimination. If we can reduce that portion of the whole, we will have made some progress. Reducing the racial ghetto to an ordinary slum, free of much of its racial tension, would mean that ordinary methods of crime prevention could be successfully utilized.

One way of doing this would be to create an escape valve which would release some of the pressures that have been building up to an explosive point. The most effective way of doing this would be to lower the walls of the ghetto to a point where those who are able to financially, can get out. But we should make certain that we do not merely create new segregated areas in the process. There is in every Negro community a large group of people who are like the citizens in every other part of our cities. They are as interested in seeing their community free from crime as any other area. But living, as they are forced to do, in a ghetto makes this next to impossible, because of overcrowded and anti-social conditions.

If such areas can be reduced to poor neighborhoods instead of segregated ghettoes, they can be dealt with the way all slums will eventually have to be dealt with, by an adequate program of education, housing, social welfare and recreation. But until we can reach that point we are merely pouring our money down the drain.

To accomplish this we will have to learn to curb our prejudices and get rid of the discriminations which grow out of them. If fiat is the only way of doing it, then we must pass anti-bias legislation with real teeth in it. This will not be accomplished overnight, nor does anyone expect it to be; but the longer we wait, the more difficult and costly will be the job. Until we can arrive at a relationship of human being to human being, there can be no solution under our present system, no matter how pious we may act or how many well-meaning interracial committees we may appoint.

## CHAPTER SIX

## THE LUXURY OF VIOLENCE

ON JUNE 20, 1943, a bill was presented to the American people. It was not the first of its kind, nor is it likely to be the last; but it was unusual in the severity of its total. The main items were prejudice and discrimination and the resultant racial tensions, plus fear and despair. Together they added up to the Detroit race riot, the worst since the East St. Louis riot of 1917. The actual cost has never been adequately measured in dollars and cents, though we know that the property loss, as in all riots, was considerable. Such violence is a luxury we can hardly afford.

The incidents leading up to June 20 are all too familiar. Detroit had been ripe for racial friction long before the war. For one thing it contained one of the worst black ghettoes in America. There are scattered islands of Negroes in almost every part of the city and its suburbs, but the majority are crowded into what is popularly called Paradise Valley. Located near Cadillac Square, it is a slum area of hastily thrown up and outmoded two-story buildings of brick or frame, exploited by white merchants and white landlords alike. Even before the influx of war workers, it was overcrowded to a point where the opening between the seams was visible to the naked eye.

The population of Detroit was 1,623,000 in 1940 but at the height of war production it was considerably larger.

# THE LUXURY OF VIOLENCE

It has been an industrial city ever since the automobile replaced the horse. When Henry Ford announced his minimum wage of five dollars a day in 1914, a wave of migration was set in motion which, save for the depression years, has been going on ever since. And that migration originated for the most part in the South, where hordes of whites and Negroes alike reacted to the new economic magnet. It has been said that one of the main troubles was that the Negroes who came North were fresh out of the cotton patch—illiterate and unused to city ways—but this was just as true of many of the whites as well.

The effect of this migration has been widespread. The truth is that to a large extent Detroit is a city of transplanted Southerners, who outnumber Negroes approximately two to one and who brought with them the mores of the region from which they came. In many ways they have attempted to force those same mores upon the whole of Detroit, and they have to a surprising extent been successful. One way in which this has been accomplished is by the usual word-of-mouth common to most Southerners; but in addition there was a camp-following of crossroads preachers, of shouters and exhorters who preached the doctrine of white supremacy along with the teachings of Jesus Christ. And always in the background hovered the shadow of the Ku Klux Klan and offshoots like the Black Legion of the early thirties and the Anglo-Saxon Federation of the present day.

In addition Detroit has been fertile ground for a number of reactionary and near-fascist groups. It was here that Father Coughlin built up his huge following, and Gerald L. K. Smith, the transplanted lieutenant of Huey Long, grew to be the No. 1 Demagogue of the nation. Nor should the Reverend J. Frank Norris be ignored, an Alabama-born, Hard Shell Baptist, who manages to serve two large con-gregations, one in Ft. Worth, Texas, and the other in Detroit, through the modern-day miracle of the aeroplane. Both Smith and Norris are racists who revolve around the old KKK hate axis—the Jew, the Negro and the Catholic—though it is interesting to note that neither is above appeal-ing to the followers of Father Coughlin when it seems to his advantage. This is the facade, but behind the scenes are an estimated twenty-five hundred Southern-born evangelists, nearly one hundred per cent reactionary racists.

This, then, was the scene in 1943—a city spoiling for a riot, a place rampant with racial tensions, where even in the midst of a war the production of fighting materiel could be halted by wildcat strikes called over the upgrad-ing of qualified Negro workers. The organized violence which attempted to stop Negroes from occupying the So-journer Truth Housing Project was another facet in the racial feelings which had been building up, almost unmo-lested, for over twenty years.

This should have been obvious, and apparently it was to almost everyone except the city authorities and the Attor-ney General of the United States. When in August of 1942 *Life* magazine exposed the latent tensions and racial dynamite in Detroit, city officials were outraged and de-nied that any such condition existed. In March of 1943 a Detroit newspaper reporter wrote Mr. Biddle, presenting the facts and what would result if precautions were not taken. The Attorney General wrote back: "Your letter has received careful attention, though it does not appear that there is sufficient evidence of violation of any Federal statute to warrant action by this department at this time." Nor did liberals, white and Negro, who visited Mayor Jeffries fare much better. The mayor was willing to listen, but what he heard seemed only to confuse him and no action of any kind was taken.

Race riots do not start by spontaneous combustion; some incident is needed to act as a detonator to set off the explosion. The people of the city of Detroit were not the only guilty ones. Every American was to blame for the prejudice which allowed a simple fist fight between a white man and a Negro in Belle Isle Park to turn into a riot barbaric enough for Nazi Germany.

That fist fight sparked off an outburst that spread first among the mixed Sunday crowd in the park and then leaped across the river, via the bridge, into the city itself. By the time police arrived it was out of hand. Two rumors quickened the spread of violence, one that a group of whites had killed a Negro woman and her baby at Belle Isle Park, the other that Negroes had raped a white woman and killed her on the park bridge. Neither was true, but by midnight the rioting had reached such proportions that local police were unable to bring it under anything remotely resembling control.

Race riots do not make pretty reading and so much has already been written * on the subject that it seems sense-

---

* One of the best, called *The Truth About the Detroit Riot* by Earl Brown, appeared in Harper's magazine late in the summer of 1943.

less to repeat all the details. The newsreels and the picture spread which appeared in *Life* magazine should have driven home to most Americans that violence is a luxury we cannot afford to repeat. But the efforts which were made to check the rioting are worth careful examination.

At four o'clock in the morning (Monday, June 21) city officials, along with army and federal authorities, were gathered in the office of the city Commissioner of Police. The Army Commander of the Detroit area said that military police could be on the scene forty-five minutes after a request was made to the proper army authorities, yet that request was not forthcoming. By six-thirty the Commissioner decided the rioting had reached a decisive break and adjourned the meeting, but at eight-thirty a Negro delegation was in the mayor's office pleading for federal troops. A half hour later the Commissioner of Police was making the same request. But when Detroit's mayor called the governor that gentleman was loath to comply since it would mean declaring martial law.

The same indecision went on until six-thirty that evening when the mayor appealed to Detroit citizens via the radio to stop rioting and declared semi-martial law. An hour later he made a tour of the city and discovered that the situation was completely out of hand, a fact which should have been apparent hours earlier, and called on the governor for help. At nine-thirty military police were on the scene and a phone call to the President of the United States brought forth a proclamation by radio at midnight. The next morning six thousand soldiers moved in and shortly afterwards order was finally restored.

# THE LUXURY OF VIOLENCE

In the meantime twenty-five Negroes and nine whites had been killed, hundreds injured and a property loss suffered amounting to hundreds of thousands of dollars.

Though Negroes suffered the greatest loss by death and injury, more Negroes were arrested than whites. Moreover it has been well established by impartial observers that in the early stages of the rioting police actually turned their backs while groups of whites slugged and beat Negroes unconscious.

Who was to blame? When the Mayor's Interracial Peace Board urged that a grand jury investigate, the city prosecutor claimed that although he did not fear such an investigation he did not favor it. Failing to notice the presence of a reporter, he went on to blame the whole riot on the National Association for the Advancement of Colored People and the local Negro newspaper. Later he denied having said any such thing.

One is reminded of the editorial which appeared in a Mississippi newspaper shortly afterward. Congressman Boykin of Alabama thought well enough of it to read it into the *Congressional Record*. Barely able to control his glee the editor wrote: "In Detroit, a city noted for the growing impudence and insolence of the Negro population, an attempt was made to put your preachments into practice. Blood on your hands, Mrs. Roosevelt, and the damned spots won't wash off, either."

Since it is evident that trouble was foreseen in Detroit and no doubt can be recognized elsewhere, there must be some technique for controlling such mob action before it gets out of hand. Three plans * have appeared recently and they are worth careful study. Each is excellent and closely enough in agreement to make possible a condensation and merger of basic ideas.

Any city with a large Negro population should determine through surveys the high points of racial tension in their community, then by every possible means attempt to lessen that tension. Police should be given special training, not only in how to handle mobs but also in the day to day problems of helping Negroes and whites to get along together. Whenever possible additional Negroes should be placed on the police force with equal ratings and opportunity for advancement. When police act fairly and intelligently, racial incidents seldom develop into riots, especially when adequate police protection arrives on the scene at once.

City authorities should keep a constant check on racial tensions all over the city, and if any trouble develops the troubled area should be shut off at once and as many of the people already in the area drained off as possible. If those who remain are broken up into smaller units it is easier for police to control them so that trouble is decentralized. Rumors play an important rôle in spreading riots; well-qualified citizens should be ready to spike falsehood at once, via radio or sound trucks. Lastly, there should be plans made for calling out the militia on short order if this proves necessary.

---

* *Why Race Riots?* by Earl Brown: Public Affairs Committee. *Race Riots Aren't Necessary* by Alfred McClung Lee: Public Affairs Committee. *Race Riots Can Be Prevented* by Ernest A. Gray: Harper's Magazine.

---

# THE LUXURY OF VIOLENCE

Such techniques have been proven workable. Their effectiveness was much in evidence in the Harlem disturbances of 1943, where a rumor that a white policeman had shot and killed a Negro soldier in a Harlem hotel came close to setting off racial dynamite. A huge crowd gathered outside the hotel and police headquarters was alerted; a large police force arrived promptly and soon Negro leaders—Walter White, Max Yergan and Ferdinand Smith—were touring the streets in sound trucks broadcasting the true facts to Harlem citizens. Hoodlums did a great deal of looting and there were some casualties, but the important thing is that racial friction was kept to a minimum.

Much the same results were observed in Washington in May of 1943. The Committee on Jobs for Negroes in Public Utilities planned an open-air mass meeting for May 8, but rumors started to flow and racial tensions developed to a point where many whites urged the chief of police to cancel the permit for the meeting. This the chief of police refused to do, stating that it would be a violation of civil rights. Instead he posted a heavy police convoy along the line of march and instructed police to maintain order in an impartial manner. The chief himself marched with the parade and there was no trouble.

A somewhat similar incident occurred in Houston, Texas, during the annual Emancipation Day parade in 1943. Rumors were widespread that Negroes planned an uprising during the celebration. The city authorities heard about this and issued a proclamation signed by an interracial committee of prominent citizens, the mayor and the chief of police. It stated that the celebration would be held as planned, and that anyone who interfered would be promptly arrested. Full-page ads to this effect were placed in both white and colored city newspapers. There was no trouble; it was one of the most smoothly functioning parades in the city's history.

Race riots can be controlled, but after all is this enough? All our elaborate precautions seem if anything an admission that we accept such violence as inevitable. It is almost a defeatist attitude, an advertisement that we are powerless to do more than appoint interracial committees and hope that somehow they will be able to isolate the violence we seem at a loss to eliminate.

The basic cause of race riots is deeply ingrained and resembles a festering sore. That sore is the result of segregation and quasi-segregation, and an inferior status which is nation-wide. We are told that this is the only way to keep the hairline balance of tension under control, yet actually this seems true neither in the North nor the South. The real effect is rather to dam up an increasing pressure and hope that it will never reach the bursting point. But this is mere wishful thinking. The longer we delay the more violent will be the explosion, for Negroes are as determined to break down the walls of segregation as whites seem to be to maintain them. The situation appears to resemble an irresistible force rushing toward an immovable object.

It is quite evident that, unless something gives, we are in for a bad time of it. Every now and then, as we have seen, something does give. Sometimes it is the logical give and take of social change, and for the moment tensions ease off; but more often the breach is from the other direction and we have another repetition of the riots which seem so integral a part of our history. So long as tensions bred of inferior status and reinforced by segregation exist, we are never safe from the possibility of violence, whatever our precautions.

There are those who claim that the so-called Negro problem is only economic. It is true that it is the result of economic exploitation and is artificially maintained on many levels for further exploitation. In the process, however, it has taken on complications which are so deeply rooted that they resemble a mental illness. And unless we undergo a social change so radical as to control social behavior by law, we shall have to eradicate them the hard way. This should not be necessary under the democratic process, which guarantees full rights to all peoples. But our history in relation to the Negro has hardly been a democratic one, save in a very few instances. So long as we shut Negroes off from the main stream of American life, whatever the reason, all that we may do for them on the banks of that river will not alter that basic fact, nor will it more than momentarily lull the familiar tensions Even if it were possible, under the status quo, to put every Negro in a decent home, each child in a separate but equal school, assure all proper medical, dental and mental care and even give a measure of economic security to the whole group, there would still be a Negro problem. Until we change that attitude and modify our resistance to integration, by whatever means, the Negro problem will be more than a minority problem and more than an economic problem. More than that, every minority group in the nation will suffer accordingly.

## CHAPTER SEVEN

## ARE TWO ARMIES BETTER THAN ONE?

THE DECLARED POLICY of the American Army in relation to the Negro soldier is perfectly clear: he is to receive the same treatment, wages and rations as white troops; and he is to have equal opportunities for recreation. This has a familiar ring, for it resembles the policy of "Separate but Equal" which we found in the South and it works out with much the same results—a loss in economy and efficiency and, however sincerely administered, something short of equality. In wages there is equality, on the surface, and much the same can be said of rations. It is officially true as to treatment, though not always so in practice. In recreation, in most areas, it is almost never true.

Enforcing such a policy, moreover, places an additional strain all the way down the line. Waging a war successfully means utilizing every available bit of manpower to its fullest extent and with the least strain on the national economy. Duplication of facilities, as we have already seen, is never economical, and whenever soldiers feel that they are being discriminated against the lowering of morale hardly makes for efficiency. It is quite true that we have never lost a war, but on several occasions, had the balance tipped only a fraction, the result might have been different. Under these circumstances does it seem wise to continue a policy which is wasteful and inefficient as well?

The problem of how best to utilize Negroes in the armed services is nothing new. Actually it existed as far back as the American Revolution. The fact is not always mentioned in our history books, but there were a number of Negroes among our early patriots. They were fully as much a part of our revolutionary heritage as any white man. Free Negroes for the most part, they took the words contained in the Declaration of Independence seriously and were eager to take part in the struggle to make them an actuality. But it seems that then, even as now, some whites were not eager that they should do so. In fact a resolution was introduced and passed by the Continental Congress early in 1775 barring any Negro from serving in the army.

The enemy was quick to see the weakness in this position and exploited it to the full. Lord Dunmore issued a public proclamation granting freedom to any American slave, capable of bearing arms, who would desert his master and make his way through to the British lines.

The number of slaves who took advantage of this offer must have been considerable, for late in the same year General George Washington reversed the position. He issued an order permitting free Negroes to enlist, and at his insistence the Congress approved it in 1776. Later the various states acted on their own initiative and several passed further legislation granting freedom to any slave who was willing to take up arms against the British. It is interesting to note that Georgia and South Carolina, both strongholds of slavery, were unwilling to make such

69

compromises and were the last areas to be freed from enemy domination. Both states were forced to utilize a large portion of their military potential to guard against the wholesale desertion of slaves, and by this dissipation of manpower were certainly less efficient than they otherwise might have been.

It does not seem that the Army learned much from this experience, for at the beginning of the War of 1812 a similar policy excluding Negroes from the Army was adopted. With the exception of two regiments of free Negroes left over from the Revolutionary War, no colored soldiers were utilized until the Battle of New Orleans. At that time General Andrew Jackson found himself far outnumbered and, in spite of the opposition of most whites, called for volunteers among the city's free men of color. In the battle which followed three battalions of newly recruited Negro soldiers were probably the deciding factors in a victory of real strategic importance.

In the Civil War the Confederacy, for obvious reasons, made almost no use of Negroes, freed men or slaves. The Union forces began with much the same policy though the results were not long in making themselves felt. The South won a series of quick victories and, had she been able to utilize all her manpower before the North's ability to produce tipped the scales, the results might have been different, for the North was badly divided and, without the Negro, far from mobilized in the early stages of the fighting.

Up until 1862 the thousands of slaves who came over to the Union lines were merely treated as contraband, placed in detention camps, or at most used as labor brigades.

70

However, in August of that year, after strong pressure from both white and Negro liberals, President Lincoln initiated the enrollment of Negroes in the Northern army. It is estimated that a quarter of a million fought against the South, the majority of them escaped slaves. As soldiers, as spies, and as a Fifth Column within the South, their contribution to the winning of the war was of vast importance.

Even in the Confederacy there had been a small minority of men like General Patrick R. Cleburne who early saw the advantage of granting freedom to all slaves who were willing to fight against the North. Their logic was that it was far better to lose even a majority of the region's slaves than to lose the independence of the South, but few were willing to listen. By the closing moments of the struggle, however, even Robert E. Lee became convinced that they were right. But by that time it was too late to put the policy into operation.

From this point on in our military history the Army never tried to get along without the Negro in wartime, but it made certain that he would be relegated to a position of inferiority. In the Spanish American War this was little more than a nebulous and unofficial policy, but in World War I it became an accepted fact. There were more Negro officers than there had ever been before, but segregation policies were very sharply defined. In a short war it is seldom possible for those who oppose such policies, within the army and without, to effect much of a change in official attitudes. Moreover, the military mind is almost universal in the belief that what was good enough to win the last war will be as effective in the next.

Thus, even before Pearl Harbor, the racial policy toward soldiers of color was firmly established. And though Negroes were eventually to serve in every branch of the services (on a segregated basis) there were times when it seemed as though they were fighting two battles—one against the enemy and the other against white America to have a chance to prove themselves against the real enemy.

If this policy of the Army in relation to the Negro soldier is so wasteful and inefficient, why have we clung to it for so long? To say that it is only because a vicious, wilful handful of Southern racists in the Army demand it, is an oversimplification. Actually there were men in high command who had been working for a change in policy, but they were slowed by the theory, also prevalent in the South, that to act too quickly would increase racial tensions to a point where they would seriously interfere with the successful prosecution of the war.

Perhaps there is some truth in this, though it seems doubtful; but this much we do know: under the racial policy in common usage racial tensions often reached a point where open hostilities broke out. Most often this seemed to be because it is impossible to carry out a policy of equality within the framework of segregation. Negroes resent this, and whites, knowing that there is a pattern of prejudice to fall back on, refuse to give an inch and are even openly hostile to any assertion on the part of colored soldiers of rights that are legally theirs.

The matter of unequal recreational facilities has caused considerable friction, both at home and abroad. We are less conscious of it here perhaps, yet it does exist, particularly in the South where rigid patterns of segregation exist in the community. Even when a segregated camp is equal so far as recreational facilities are concerned, there is little real equality once a Negro soldier is off the limits of the post. In the near-by town he is limited in the places he may go to eat, the movies he may attend, and in fact all the little things which help to make army life bearable. Even more important our transportation facilities place a real hardship on a soldier whose skin happens to be black. Going to and from town, busses which are crowded usually refuse to stop for Negro service men and most taxis will not carry colored fares. The result is that Negro soldiers may be late in checking in or have to cut short whatever recreation they may be enjoying in order to be certain of checking in on time. This is hardly equality of recreation.

When American troops are sent abroad it is interesting to note their attempts to impose upon others their way of doing things. This has been especially true of racial mores, where patterns of segregation have not existed until we imported them and where prejudice toward Negroes was no part of the people's thinking. It was a common thing for white soldiers to go out of their way to break up the normal fraternization between Negroes and white Europeans. Sometimes this was successful, more often not. Our Negro troops were popular with civilians, especially children. In fact, as Roi Ottley points out, the European peasant and the English working man have much in common with the Negro. In the case of the peasant there is a common tie with the soil; and the working-class Britisher has not enjoyed the unusually high standard of living so common in America, being on an economic and environ-

73

mental basis more closely akin to the colored than the white American.

When troops came into a new area, it was not uncommon for white officers to go into the nearest town and pick out the best recreational facilities for white troops, leaving little if anything for Negro soldiers. In such cases those places set aside for whites were declared out of bounds to Negroes. In other instances certain nights were set aside for white soldiers to go to town, different nights for Negroes. The result was nothing but the most obvious kind of discrimination toward Negro troops.

Nor has the Red Cross been without blame in this respect. One hesitates to castigate an organization which has such worthy objectives, but the truth is that the Red Cross has in many instances been a more rigid upholder of jim crow than the Army itself. Naturally the business of trying to solve the race problem is not within the province of such an organization, but the welfare of all humanity most certainly is.

And in the segregation of blood plasma the Red Cross has been guilty of more than a reactionary policy. To point out that the whole program for the storing and distribution of blood plasma was originated by Dr. Charles Drew, a Negro, makes such a policy even more paradoxical. It is doubtful indeed that a wounded man is going to worry about whether the blood he is about to receive came from a white or a colored man, especially since science tells us that there is no difference in the blood of any person, regardless of race, creed or color. Blood differs only in type and each type appears in the blood of all peoples.

Yet the Red Cross, by following a policy of segregated

blood banks, would seem to prefer the scientific findings of Congressman John Rankin of Mississippi, who claimed that not to separate plasma was a communist plot to mongrelize America. Said Mr. Rankin: "They wanted to pump Negro or Japanese blood into the veins of our wounded white boys regardless of the dire effect it might have on their children."

That there could be no effect was quickly pointed out and in a manner that no literate man could fail to understand. Certainly this policy was dangerous; it limited the supply of available plasma and hardly added to the homefront morale of Negroes whose sons were fighting on all fronts.

These are but some of the instances which show that under segregation, no matter how honorable intentions may be, it is impossible to have equality. Furthermore, directives from the top are not always obeyed. Local conditions vary, and there will always be those quick to take advantage of a situation. The duplication of facilities which are part of segregation also cost taxpayers more than they might otherwise pay. Yet if this had assured a maximum of efficiency in our fighting potential, it might have been wise to forego change so long as a crisis existed, but the unwieldiness of replacements alone denies this.

The facts seem to be otherwise. At least they are open to doubt. The number of instances of conflicts between white and Negroes in the armed services, and white civilians and Negro soldiers on the homefront, does not tend to bear out the contention of lessened racial tensions. Such clashes between civilians and soldiers occurred mainly in the South, where whites simply refused to respect the uniform of the United States Army when worn by a Negro. Moreover, in no case did Army authorities take action against such civilians, although they were clearly disrupting the war effort.

In the armed forces, conflicts between whites and Negroes ranged all the way from minor fist fights between individuals or small groups to actual armed strife. In Lancaster, England, the shooting of two Negroes by a white MP in a minor fracas set off a pitched battle between white and Negro troops. Nor were such conflicts limited to the Army alone. Much the same thing happened in the Navy, limited mainly to sitdown strikes in the distaff divisions of the WAAC and the WAVES. In the Coast Guard, which observes only a token segregation, such incidents have been at a minimum.

Thus it would seem that the magical safety valve of segregation has not kept racial tensions under control the way those who support it claim it should. The main reason for this, in the minds of many observers, is the undeniable fact that, so long as such a policy is maintained, those whites who are prejudiced feel complete security against punishment.

Actually there is data, though on a limited scale, to show that when the bars of segregation are lowered racial tensions do decrease. Toward the end of the war it was apparent that there were some in authority who were conscientiously trying to eliminate the discriminatory practices and even modify jim crow policies all along the line. For one thing Negroes were serving in every branch of the services and on a minor scale earning better ratings than Negroes had ever before attained. Such progress was not limited to any branch of the service, though it varied widely in degree.

One fact which impressed many observers was that, the nearer one got to the actual fighting zone, the less rigid seemed to be the barriers of segregation. This was nothing which could be traced to official policy, but merely seemed the quite natural reaction of men who were too busy fighting to bother about such nonsense. Actually it was possible to follow the disintegration of segregation as one neared the battle line.

But there were other segments of the Army not in battle areas where jim crow was not in effect. In Officer Candidate Schools, for example, trainees took their alphabetical place in formations, hutments and classes, regardless of race, creed or color. No one seemed to find fault with this arrangement. No race riots resulted, because the policy was firm and understood. The Army was saved the expense of providing separate accommodations and also the need of defending them if it had.

But perhaps the most telling experiment occurred in the closing months of the war and on a large enough scale to show rather conclusively that an army can function effectively without rigid segregation. In the winter of 1944, during the final push on the Western Front, a call went out for volunteers to serve in mixed divisions. Several thousand Negroes volunteered and it is worth mentioning that by doing so all of them lost their ratings. Two thousand six hundred were accepted as qualified and given six weeks of intensive combat training (many were from service units, the main utilization of Negroes in this war). Finally they were formed into rifle platoons super-imposed on the normal company complement of one heavy-weapons platoon plus three rifle platoons. Thus one of these colored rifle platoons entered every infantry regiment in a division, eleven divisions in all being affected.

This is far from a complete breakdown of segregation but it is the nearest thing to it that the Army had ever attempted. All the officers were white, and so were the majority of non-commissioned officers. A survey made at the end of two months of actual fighting shows some significant results.

Asked at the start of the experiment if they liked the idea of serving with Negroes, 64 per cent declared that they did not and only 34 per cent said they were willing to give it a try. The remaining 2 per cent did not have an opinion either way. At the end of two months, however, these same whites had more or less reversed their original stand. None of them, when asked how they got along with colored troops, answered "not so well." Of the officers 7 per cent and of the non-coms 36 per cent replied "fairly well"; 73 per cent of the officers and 60 per cent of the non-coms answered "very well." The rest had no opinion.

Upon being asked how the Negro troops fought, none answered "not well at all," and only 1 per cent said "fairly well." Sixteen per cent of the officers and 17 per cent of the non-coms replied "well," and 84 per cent of the officers and 81 per cent of the non-coms answered "very well." Furthermore, when queried if their racial attitudes had been affected by this experiment, no white replied that he had received a negative impression and 77 per cent answered that their attitudes had undergone a change for the better. In both instances a negligible percentage made no reply.

"When I heard about it," a white sergeant from South Carolina stated, "I said I'd be damned if I'd wear the same shoulder patch they did. After that first day when we saw how they fought, I changed my mind. They're just like any of the other boys to us."

The Army also must have undergone a change in thinking, for on the 3rd of May of this year a new policy was announced regarding the Negro soldier. In short, it will mean the breakup of the usual Negro infantry divisions, such as the Ninety-second and Ninety-third, into regiments composed of approximately 2,700 men, which will then be combined with white regiments to form mixed units of division strength. Since the policy grew out of a three-man report prepared by Lieutenant General Alvin C. Gillam which stressed the "eminent success" of Negro platoons in white companies, it is assumed that the basic mixed units will be companies and in no case will the mixing be below the platoon level. The report also states that more Negro officers are to be upgraded and new ones commissioned, particularly those with World War II experience. Also recommended is the principle that Negro troops be stationed in localities where community attitudes are more favorable and in such strength as will not constitute an undue burden on the local civilian population, except where military necessity and the interest of national security dictate otherwise.

While such a reversal of policy is heartening it is regrettable that it does not go farther. Actually the word "segregation" is not once mentioned in the report and though it is implied that the Army is working toward the eventual end of all jim crow, mixed units of platoon strength are in effect quasi-segregation and no solution to the basic problem. Certainly the provision that Negro troops are not to be stationed in the South is a wise one, but one wonders what will happen when military necessity and the interest of national security dictate otherwise. If in such an emergency government or army authority takes a firm stand—possibly to the extent of declaring that it will be a civil offense when civilians show prejudice or discrimination toward *any* soldier wearing the uniform of the United States Army—well and good; if not we are right back where we started.

In fact a firm stand was actually called for by the Selective Service Act, which stated that in the selection and training of men under said act there should be no discrimination against any person on account of race or color. Whether such a policy was actually enforceable no one knows, because the Army made no effort to find out. Indeed, had there been a presidential proclamation stating that there was no time for the foolishness of racial prejudice and discrimination in a total war, the race problem might have been largely solved so far as the Army was concerned. A civilian may kick Negroes around and get away with it, but the same man as a soldier, knowing that by so doing he will face court-martial, will not be so eager to indulge himself. And in the process he might learn that fighting side by side with Negroes while defending his country does not, of necessity, mean that his sister will be forced to marry a Negro, either while he is away fighting or after he gets back.

Actually there is something very fundamental at stake and there is little use in trying to side-step the issue. The Gillam report stresses that Negro soldiers were most successful in small units employed in close association with white units on similar tasks. What it does not point out, save by inference, is that large, segregated Negro infantry units under white officers were for the most part a failure. There were so many instances in the recent war of individual bravery and resourcefulness among Negroes that to assume such failures were due to cowardliness is sheer nonsense. In quasi-mixed units Negroes more than carried their share of the fighting.

What, then, is the answer to the poor record of some Negro troops in the Italian campaign? Certainly it was not, as some claimed, that Negro soldiers were so afraid of ghosts and haunts that they "melted away" after dark. Nor is the whole answer to be found in higher illiteracy rates and improper training. That both were parts of the answer will be apparent to anyone who bothers to study the differentials in Negro-white educational facilities, but actually it goes deeper than that.

The all-white command of such troops was primarily made up of white Southerners who cared not one whit whether or not their men were successful. For the most part they looked upon such a command as a sort of punishment, on a level with being banished to Siberia or the outer provinces. But the real blame for what failures there were, can be placed squarely on the prejudice of white Americans at home as well as in the Army.

81

# THE HIGH COST OF PREJUDICE

For eighty years Negroes have been kicked around, and the psychological effects of such treatment have never been measured. When Negroes got in the Army they found the basic pattern little changed. This was the Negro's war as much as ours, and he knew it; but he wanted to fight that war as a man and not as a second- or third-class citizen. Instead he was forced to fight two battles, one against the enemy and the other against white American prejudice. As a result he was bitter, badly conditioned, robbed of his pride and his manhood.

That is not the material out of which to build a soldier, without first giving him something to fight for. It is more than that in fact, it is the most wasteful sort of inefficiency in the utilization of manpower. No nation can afford to have one man out of ten in its military potential made largely ineffective by the prejudices of our national life. To continue to do so is plain stupidity.

## CHAPTER EIGHT

## *REPRESENTATIVES WHO REPRESENT NOBODY*

THE SOUTHERN demagogue is one way in which the South pays for its prejudices. He is the end result of ignorance and poverty, of white supremacy and voting restrictions. He plays on the bigotry of his constituents and, like the old-style medicine man, he puts on a good show with all the trimmings. It even seems on the surface that he has the full support of the folks back home, but thanks to the poll tax, the white primary, the intimidation of Negro voters and the difficulties of registration, he is actually a representative who represents nobody.

A little quick arithmetic will prove the truth of this statement. Senator Bilbo, who supposedly speaks for the people of Mississippi, was re-elected in 1942 by 4 per cent of the potential vote and 2 per cent of the state population. The South Carolinian Burnet R. Maybank was sent back to Washington in the same year by 2 per cent of the potential vote and only 1 per cent of the population. And Harry F. Byrd of Virginia received 19 per cent of the potential vote from 11 per cent of the population in the 1940 elections. One could go on, but this is enough to make the point.

The contrast with the free-voting states is striking. In 1944, for example, it has been estimated that 57 per cent of the potential voters in states without voting restrictions went to the polls, while the average of the eight Southern poll-tax states was a mere 19 per cent of potential. Nor is this all, for even in those Southern states where the poll tax has been repealed—Georgia, Louisiana, North Carolina, Florida and Kentucky—the hangover from that restriction has made many voters lethargic to the ballot. Only an educational campaign will make them realize, not only that they can vote, but why it is to their advantage to do so. And though the Supreme Court decision, recently reaffirmed, which opens the white primary to Negro voters will have a decided bearing toward freeing the South of the demagogue, the indications from this summer's primaries are that its full effect may not be felt at once.

Actually the prejudice responsible for such legislators has resulted in far more costly items than the buffoonery and hysterical rantings which make most decent-thinking Southerners wince. The truth is that the whole cultural and intellectual pattern necessary to "keeping the Negro in his place" has made possible reaction and chicanery throughout the whole political scene in the South. It has meant the one-party system, which has blocked political progress in the region. It has kept many good candidates from seeking office, because they hesitated to compete with the rabble-rousers on the race-baiting level to which such men stooped in seeking office. And even if on occasion a decent-thinking man took the chance, he was forced into a variation of this technique or his chances of election were slim indeed.

The reason given for voting restrictions in the South has been the threat of black domination, though actually a survey shows that in no state would black voters out-number whites. Only in isolated counties does this threat have any true substance in fact. Yet, true or false, it has been responsible for the boycott of more legislation than any other single factor in the whole panarama of our national life.

The prejudice of the South against Negroes has also kept the South backward in still another way. It has been the wedge which split the only two progressive movements the South has ever experienced. And at the present time, from all appearances, those same forces are at work in an attempt to split the Democratic Party, though the chances are that the less progressive splinter is likely to cut its own throat in the process.

After the Civil War a victorious North imposed Reconstruction on a defeated South. We are not concerned here with ethics, but what is of interest is the fact that for the first time whites and Negroes had a chance to work together toward a common end. New state constitutions were drafted, in many instances by white and Negro delegates. A free school system which was the forerunner of the public school systems in the South today was put into operation and laws regarding a more liberal attitude toward debtors were enacted. Divorce laws were studied and recommendations made for future action. The question of woman suffrage was hotly debated and for perhaps the first time in our history given serious consideration. Indeed, in South Carolina a bill aimed at giving the vote to women came close to passage.

The important thing is that Negroes and whites were

85

working together—if not with brotherly love, at least without too much friction. The effect which this must have had on the aristocracy is not hard to imagine, for the one thing those who had been in control feared most was that the poor white and the Negro would form common political cause. It was not long before the gentry banded themselves together and set out to wreck what had thus far been accomplished. Through the outlets which were closely controlled by the white aristocracy—press, pulpit and politics—the same message was alternately shouted and whispered in wheedling tones. Look out for black domination. There's not going to be enough to go around so you better be sure to get your share before the "nigger" does. You take care of him and we'll take care of the money. Above all, protect Southern womanhood against the threat of the black rapist.

The last was perhaps the most effective, although a Southern social historian of a later day, W. J. Cash,* has estimated the chances of a Southern white woman being violated by a Negro as considerably less than her chances of being struck by lightning. The rest is past history. Reconstruction was set aside by the compromise of 1876, and the first serious attempt of Negroes and whites to work out their differences together was defeated. And actually the reaction which set in worked almost as great a hardship upon the poor white as upon the Negro.

There was to be one more opportunity, the Southern Populist movement at the turn of the century. It was in the beginning a movement by poor whites to free them-

* *The Mind of the South* by W. J. Cash. Knopf.

selves from the political domination of the post-bellum aristocracy. Ben Tillman, a small farmer but by no stretch of the imagination a poor white, first broke the rule of the upper classes in South Carolina when he managed to defeat Wade Hampton, a former Confederate war hero, for the governorship. But this was the same Tillman who later became the infamous "Pitchfork Ben," the South's first demagogue and one of the worst Negro-baiters the United States Senate has ever seen. There had been no change in Tillman, who was a racist from the beginning, but had he been free from prejudices his story might have been written in different terms.

But under Tom Watson of Georgia, what had started out as a mere revolt against political domination by the gentry assumed the proportions of a true progressive upheaval. Watson joined forces with the Populists of the North to spearhead a drive to bring relief to all the common people in the South, black and white alike. Yet eventually both the movement and Watson were doomed to failure by the prejudice of the region and a reactionary Democratic Party who knew best how to exploit it, since they themselves had helped to create it for political purposes. The personal tragedy of Watson is that he turned from an advocate of interracial political pressures of a liberal nature into one of the worst of the racists—whether for political gain or from inner conviction it is difficult to say. But the results were the same and the South lost its second battle to reaction.

What actually happened is not unlike what has happened between the present-day liberal and reactionary wings of the Democratic Party. The old-line boys in the beginning feared Watson fully as much as the same kind of men grew to fear Roosevelt, and for much the same reasons. But the difference is that Roosevelt was strong enough to be elected without the Southern Democratic vote. Though the Populists had managed it once, they were afraid to risk it again when the heat was turned on. That heat was the race issue, and the result was the disfranchisement of the Negro and the white primary. Reaction was firmly back in the saddle once again.

Those who think that the Negro never votes in the South overlook another evil which the system has worked on itself. Or perhaps it would be more accurate to say that *Negroes are voted.* Why this has happened is but another cost of discrimination. Since Negroes have, until recently, had nothing to say about the Democratic candidate, and the Republican candidate could never win anyway, their vote was really meaningless. As a result when money or other favors were offered, some Negroes were quick to take advantage of it. The two best examples of this are the Crump machine in Shelby County, Tennessee, and the dominant political faction in San Antonio, Texas.

Shelby County, of which Memphis is the stronghold, votes Negroes regularly, so long as they vote the way Mr. Crump wants them to vote. In fact, partially through this process, Mr. Crump has been able to control the whole state of Tennessee. A rival may come into Shelby County with a comfortable lead only to go out without his shirt, or the election. If one vote per voter will not do the trick, Mr. Crump, they say, is not above having his Negroes vote several times.

# REPRESENTATIVES WHO REPRESENT NOBODY

San Antonio is little better. Corrupt white and Negro politicians control huge blocks of Negro votes because the prejudice of the South has made those votes useless. Not long ago this brought forth a ludicrous situation. A powerful Negro politician, gambler and racketeer died, and the Governor, the Mayor, a United States Senator and several Congressmen walked gravely in his funeral cortège. The solid block of Negro votes which he controlled was responsible for their being in office and would more than likely keep them there.

It is easy enough to condemn Negroes who sell their vote and by inference castigate all Negroes, but the truth is that we made that vote impotent. Nor would a corrupt Negro politician have been able to stay in power if that vote had been meaningful to those who owned it. Until very recently this has even been true in large Northern cities where, although there were no voting restrictions, Negroes voted blindly on racial lines or for the white candidate who could give them the best circus. In the end no candidate would do anything for them anyway, except appoint a few Negroes to public office as a token payment for their support. A good example of this was the reign of "Big Bill" Thompson in Chicago.

But the nearer the Negro has come to finding real value and meaning in his vote, the more intelligently he has used it. He deserted the Republican Party in 1936 because he saw real meaning in the New Deal and, though Wendell L. Willkie might have brought him back into the fold in 1944, Thomas E. Dewey couldn't. He could get the Negro vote as candidate for governor of New York state, but not as a presidential candidate.

# THE HIGH COST OF PREJUDICE

In the South the Negro vote is going to open up possibilities for better representatives, in spite of some of the results in this year's primary elections. In the North the pivotal Negro vote is already the balance of power in any national election and is likely to be the same in many state and municipal elections. When the South becomes used to the idea of Negroes voting one of the great costs of prejudice will be removed. But it is easy to think of the Southern demagogue as a regional phenomenon who hurts the South only. Actually he has his hands around the throat of the North as well under a Democratic administration.

Seniority of service is the basis for membership in all the important committees in both the House and the Senate. The chairmen of such committees wield a power which can actually hamstring the program of any administration by choking it off before it is even born. One thing our prejudices have done in the South is to put into strategic positions some of the most reactionary of Southerners. Such men head ten important committees in the Senate, seventeen in the House. Nor is this all, for in most instances the men who will succeed them might as well be their twin brothers.

On the Committee for Senate Appropriations, for example, is Carter Glass of Virginia. Walter George of Georgia heads up the Committee on Finance and in the Committee on Foreign Affairs is to be found Tom Connally of Texas. Commerce chairman is Josiah Bailey of North Carolina while the Committee on Immigration is headed by Russell of Georgia, a state not known for its hospitality to those who are not of native Anglo-Saxon stock. The powerful Rules Committee has Harry Byrd of Virginia in command. A special Committee on Post-War Economic Policy and Planning is headed by Walter George of Georgia. Nor should we ignore the Committee on the District of Columbia. As its chairman, Theodore Bilbo of Mississippi is actually the unofficial mayor of Washington.

In the House as head of the Judiciary Committee is Hatton Sumners of Texas. Military Affairs: Andrew May of Kentucky. Naval Affairs: Carl Vinson of Georgia. World War Veterans: John Rankin of Mississippi. Investigating Acts of Executive Agencies: Smith of Texas. Un-American Activities: John Wood of Georgia, a sort of Charlie McCarthy for Rankin of Mississippi.

Does this affect us all, North and South? Yes, it has resulted in the blocking of legislation not only of interest to the South but vital to the whole nation. Not all of these men are in the demagogue class, to be sure, but each of them is bound to present a solid front against any legislation even remotely approaching the color line. There has not been a major filibuster by a Northerner in a number of years—none in fact since the long and sincere attempt of the elder La Follette to keep us out of World War I. In recent years, however, the racists have made a mockery of its use.

A filibuster is simply the process of gaining the floor on a point of technical nature and blocking passage of a certain piece of legislation by talking it to death. It is usually successful because even those in favor of the bill do not like to see other important legislation held up as a result of such tactics. It was intended as a guarantee that minor-

THE HIGH COST OF PREJUDICE

ity opinion be given full opportunity to express itself, but it has seldom been used for that reason in recent years.

For the racist it has been a powerful weapon. Anti-poll tax legislation has been filibustered to death and the same has been true of anti-lynch bills, though a clear majority of both houses was in favor of both. In the recent attempt to make the Fair Employment Practices Commission a permanent body, the weapon reached a new, all time low. It was aided by the fact that Senator McKellar, Vice-President of the Senate, was presiding over the session and worked hand in glove with the filibusterers, even to the point of doubtful parliamentary procedure. The defeat of the legislation was sad enough. But while Southern demagogues drearily corrected the Senate journal comma by comma and made a farce of the whole democratic process, the business of the Senate came to a complete standstill for days, other business at hand dammed up behind a wall of non-essential oratory.

Mentioned earlier was the fact that Southern Democrats, on purely racial lines, were thwarting the clearly set policy of that party. In 1944 Mr. Roosevelt was re-elected without their aid. The things Mr. Roosevelt stood for were clear and were approved by a majority of his party.

The close collaboration of reactionary Southern Democrats and Northern Republicans is a clear case of an attempt to work against the ideals of that party and the will of the majority of the nation's voters, a costly business for the American people at large.

## CHAPTER NINE

## SALES RESISTANCE ABROAD

A RACE riot in Detroit—even a lynching in the smallest town of the deep South—sends out reverberations which are heard and felt all over the world. In varying degrees they influence our relations with the peoples of the Far East, the Malay States, India and Africa—in all two-thirds of the world's population. Normally this can be called bad public relations but in a war, especially one aimed at discouraging discrimination, it was nothing short of giving ammunition to the enemy on a silver platter.

The Japanese were not slow to take advantage of this fact. Their short-wave broadcasting stations were continually beaming to wherever colored people dwell the story of Mobile and Beaumont, of friction between white and colored soldiers in the South, of even the least important incidents where white Americans showed bias toward their fellow-citizens of darker skin. Nor was Germany slow to back up the same propaganda on her air waves, perhaps less successfully, but nonetheless with some overall effect.

How successful was this action on the part of our enemies, has yet to be fully realized. We do know that in the Malay States, where the British received a sound beating, the native population actually welcomed the Japanese as the deliverers who would get them out from under the heel of their white oppressors. That in this particular case the natives were jumping from the frying pan into the fire makes little difference; the fact remains that their resentment had been framed by the same kind of propaganda against the British that the Japs had used against us. In Indo-China the same was true, though to a lesser degree. A segment of India was openly pro-Japanese. And if the majority was not, it wasn't pro-British either. Only in the Philippines were the Japs really ineffective.

It is no overstatement to say that many colored persons in the world felt a certain elation in the early stages of the Japanese War. Only a small minority did not want an eventual Allied victory, but nonetheless there was an inner hope that victory might be difficult enough, so that the myth of the white man's superiority might suffer a little in the process.

For years all the colored peoples of the world have suffered from white exploitation, discrimination and an offensive patronage at best. The consequences of this attitude are finally beginning to catch up with us. It is one thing to aspire to be a little tin god, but it is quite another thing when after an elaborate build-up, your actions show your feet to be of clay. The world is shrinking fast through such media as the aeroplane, the radio and the atom bomb. The white man's burden is getting a little too heavy to carry, not because of the weight of that burden but because in the cold light of day the white man looks so small. It was only his shadow cast against the wall of ignorance that seemed so large and noble.

# SALES RESISTANCE ABROAD

To get closer to home: The main terminal of Pan American Air Ways is located in Miami, Florida. Though jim crow restrictions are largely non-existent on commercial airlines, they do exist at any terminal in the South. What might be the effect if a powerful foreign government happened to have a colored man as an envoy and in spite of the usual precautions of the State Department, he was jim crowed at the Miami airport? Possibly the State Department also worries about this, even when less important dignitaries arrive from the West Indies or South America.

It is difficult enough in Washington, which is in many respects as much a jim crow city as any in the deep South. Negroes are not allowed in theaters, restaurants or hotels, and they have very limited cab service. To add to the general confusion they are not, however, segregated on street cars, in the restaurant at the Union Station, or in government-operated cafeterias. Foreign envoys or even distinguished visitors must find this rather limiting.

The chances are that the State Department, when forced to find entertainment for distinguished guests who happen to be colored, finds these restrictions a bit limiting too. The Department maintains Blair-Lee House, since hotels refuse service to Negroes; but the usual procedure is to dump the whole problem into the lap of Howard University, a Negro college in Washington, which then assumes the rôle of host. How this impresses the visiting dignitaries is open to considerable doubt, particularly if they see through the rather transparent ruse. Students and faculty members of Howard have been known to mutter

95

that it keeps them too busy to carry on a normal academic schedule, and though this is spoken in jest there is enough truth in it to give us pause.

Recently the United Nations sent a committee to investigate sites for a permanent home for that organization. After some difficulties New York City was chosen as a temporary site and several recommendations were made for the future. One thing which probably restricted the choice was that such a site could not be located in any area which had legal jim crow ·restrictions. An insult to some delegate might have world repercussions, not to mention the paradox of trying to deal democratically with world problems in a region where the most rigid sort of discrimination is practiced.

Recently the members of the World Bank met in Savannah, Georgia. It took a government directive, at the instigation of the National Association for the Advancement of Colored People, to make certain no unlikely incident took place in the hotel where the delegates were stopping.

These are some of the more obvious ways in which prejudice and discrimination tend to give us bad public relations in the world at large. Certainly the situation in India has made bad publicity for the British Empire all over the world, in spite of the fact that the split between Moslem and Hindu is a complex problem difficult of solution.

The amount of money that big business spends each year on public relations must be money well spent, or hard-headed industrialists would not continue the process year after year. During the war the Office of War Information expended large sums to sell America throughout the world. Our color line made this a tough job, since it had made billions of people suspicious of us and cynical toward the Four Freedoms, which, the world knows, do not wholly apply either in America or the British Empire. People know that fact from bitter experience.

But by no means are all those who put up sales resistance colored peoples. Some of them are our own allies. It is alleged that President Roosevelt once told Prime Minister Churchill that the true facts about the English colonial system should be exposed to the pitiless spotlight of world opinion. Mr. Churchill's answer was brief but to the point: "And when you do, Mr. President, will you turn that same spotlight on Georgia?"

Again, when Mr. Byrnes was lecturing the Russians about democratic elections in the Balkans it is said that they told him frankly, and to his face, that his native state of South Carolina for a quarter of a century had never raised a voice against the poll tax or other schemes which effectively kept Negroes from exercising their right to vote. Further, they asked him how he could prattle about democracy when he himself had retained his seat in the Senate by as undemocratic and corrupt a political system as existed in the world? Mr. Byrnes, it is reported, had no effective answer.

One of our post-war projects is for the continuation, in peacetime, of at least some of the functions of the Office of War Information. Under State Department supervision, William Benton will attempt to reach areas of the world which know very little about America and explain to them what kind of people we are and how we carry on our

97

national life. This makes good sense; it is easier to do business with someone when he knows who you are and how you think and feel. Through its regular channels the State Department cannot perform this function and has often found its diplomatic effectiveness curtailed as a result. But on our past record the handicaps of our prejudice may well limit the success of such a project.

At the core of our bad relations with two-thirds of the world is the colonial question. Actually Great Britain is the worst offender of all, but the unpleasant truth is that we are lumped in with all the white oppressors. Our attitude toward peoples with darker skins is well known, and at the present time most colonials fall into this category. Although this was not always true, our prejudiced minds are quick to associate this with the fallacy that such people are inferior. Because they do not now measure up to our standards of progress they will never be able to, we say, and consequently the white man is justified in keeping them under his heel.

This, of course, is pure nonsense, the fallacy being that civilization is an equation of relativity. Because we were strong enough in offensive technique to grab off colonies does not of necessity mean that we are individually stronger in body, keener of mind or even basically more cultured. We are fond of calling any civilization which is not wholly mechanized a primitive one, which is far from true in many cases. Again we find ourselves in the realm of legends and myths.

Men who feel guilty inside must justify themselves before their fellow-men. But the myth of the white man's burden no longer bears cold scrutiny. The reasons for colonies are purely economic in nature. It wasn't that we wanted to bring the fruits of our superior culture to misguided savages. In the sixteenth century colonies brought in more to the governments which exploited them than it cost to run them. Today this is no longer true, but colonies are still profitable because they offer private investment capital earnings out of all proportion to those realized at home. The result is exploitation and slave wages, administration by white men often incapable of maintaining themselves in the competition of the home country, and a solid front against too rapid social change in colonial areas.

Perhaps this financial gain has been worth it to the handful of persons most selfishly concerned, but something very precious has been lost in the process. The ruthless and ignorant destruction of cultural folk patterns, for example, and the violation of a people's moral standard. Those who maintain that colonizers brough improved health standards might better add that this was solely because the European found it impossible to live without better public health administration. But even so the loss of life largely outweighs these gains. In French Equitorial Africa there were twenty million natives at the turn of the century, only eight millions by 1921, and a scarce three millions by 1934.

In exchange for this financial gain—just how large no one really knows—we have put ourselves in the hopeless moral position of trying to justify something for which there is no real justification. Mr. Churchill may thunder that he was not put into the position of Prime Minister

99

to sit in at the breakup of his Majesty's government. Now he no longer is in that position, and the pressures toward a solution of the colonial question are more strongly compelling than ever before.

Indeed, we of the white world are growing weaker the longer we try to maintain our colonial position, while those we are holding in oppression are growing stronger. The Four Freedoms was our pledge of action, yet we have done nothing but hold fast to the status quo. We have lost prestige in Greece, in Indonesia and the Middle East, where havenot-nationals, colonials, and natives wonder if our brave words about those freedoms were not, as usual, uttered in mockery.

In a recent book * Walter White, Executive Secretary of the National Association for the Advancement of Colored People, summed up the results of his trip around the world: "A wind is rising—a wind of determination by the havenots to share the benefits of freedom and prosperity which the haves of the world have tried to keep exclusively for themselves. That wind blows all over the world. Whether that wind develops into a hurricane is a decision which we must make now and in the days when we form the peace."

There is one lesson we should have learned from the recent war, and if we have not learned it the storm signals will be out for the future. That lesson is the simple fact that if Japan had not been an aggressive. fascist, military dictatorship, she could have had two-thirds of the world

---

* A Rising Wind by Walter White. Doubleday.

fighting on her side. Such a realization should give us pause for deep thinking.

It is no longer true that the darker peoples of the earth are our inferiors and cannot be educated to take their place with us as equals in a free world. This is sheer nonsense as great numbers of them, when given the chance, have already proven. Everywhere there is a restless stirring throughout the world and, though we may be able to maintain our position of supposed superiority against those pressures for some time, eventually we will be faced with aggressive action along purely color lines. There is no way of knowing now whether this could lead the world into another war, but the possibility exists. Were it to happen, Russia would be found aligning herself with the darker peoples of the world.

Leaving out entirely our feelings toward the system of government which Russia has, our own prejudices may force two-thirds of the world into a close cooperation with Russia against us. We often tell ourselves that it is impossible to change the mores of a country by fiat, yet Russia, with a deeply ingrained anti-Semitic background, has accomplished this by outlawing prejudice and discrimination by statute. This factor is of great significance all over the world and wherever a minority suffers from prejudice and discrimination.

Our prejudices stand in the way of our arriving at a mutual understanding with all of the peoples of the world. We by no means have that trust now; and all our attempts to gain it are going to become increasingly futile, until we have broken down the sales resistance of two-thirds of the world by removing the factor most responsible for it.

## CHAPTER TEN

# WHAT DOESN'T SHOW ON THE BALANCE SHEET

NOT ALL of the high costs of prejudice show up on the balance sheet. There is very little available data, for example, on those who have left very prejudiced areas because of discrimination. We do know that the rural districts of the South usually export about a fourth of their natural increase in sons and daughters, some to urban centers of the South but a large percentage to the North. This migration has taken from the South many of its ablest people, exactly how many no one knows. It has been estimated, however, that almost half of the well-known scientists born in the South are now living elsewhere and we have noted too the large proportion of Southerners in the large industrial centers of the North such as Detroit.

But breaking down such figures into a meaningful pattern is next to impossible. The best one can do is surmise and generalize, for even the causes for such migration are not always clear. The need for whites to find greater opportunities than are available in the overcrowded, economically underdeveloped Southern community would not on the surface seem to be the result of prejudice. Yet actually we do not really know the extent to which "keeping the Negro in his place" contributes to holding the white as well on a low economic plane. If it is not possible to say that there is a direct bearing, at least there seems to be an indirect one.

In the case of the Negro, however, the results of prejudice are clear enough. There is no doubt that the cream of the Negro population has moved North in search of better job opportunities and a measure of freedom from the rigid and lawful discriminations of the South. In recent years a slight improvement in employment, particularly in academic circles, has caused a small minority to gravitate back, but the majority remain in the North where they contribute in a variety of ways to the well-being of the community. The fact that they have left the South is a real loss to the region, and many white Southerners are well aware of the fact.

Examples appear in all walks of life. There have been artists, writers, actors, doctors, athletes, educators and lawyers who could have contributed a great deal to the South, had they not been driven from the area by discrimination. That this has been costly to the South seems obvious.

But almost as many whites have left the South, and though many of them have done so merely because of better jobs, others left because they could no longer tolerate the prejudices and discriminations which made of their homeland a backward and bigoted area. Some have written books in which they have minced no words in stating their feelings; others have merely been content to find new places in which to live.

Supposedly the University of North Carolina is at work on a project to gather data on the number of important white citizens who have left the South and their reasons

103

for doing so. The results should be interesting, though it seems doubtful if anything significant concerning prejudice will be turned up by such a questionnaire.

One thing does seem clear, however, and that is that no region can long afford to be bled dry of its best talent, whatever its race, creed or color. Mediocrity will be the inevitable result.

Marian Anderson, the outstanding contralto, was refused the use of Constitution Hall in Washington in 1940 on the grounds that the singer was a Negro. A storm of protest greeted this action, and when Harold L. Ickes, then Secretary of the Interior, suggested that Miss Anderson sing on the steps of the Washington Monument, a mixed audience of seventy-five thousand turned out to listen. But the fact remains that prejudice very nearly robbed thousands of an experience which would have greatly enriched their lives.

Nor is this an isolated case. At a later date the hall was also refused Hazel Scott, concert pianist and wife of A. Clayton Powell, Jr., New York Congressman, on the same grounds. Many Negro artists flatly refuse to appear before segregated audiences and with good reason. Paul Robeson on one occasion in Kansas City startled his audience by interrupting himself in the midst of a concert to make the following statement:

"I have made it a lifelong habit to refuse to sing in Southern states, or anywhere that audiences are segregated. I accepted this engagement under the guarantee that there would be no segregation. Since many local leaders of my own race have urged me to fulfil this engagement, I shall finish this concert, but I am doing so under protest."

An increasing number of colored artists are taking the same stand, which, so far as the South is concerned, certainly constitutes a great cultural loss. The sad experiences of most Negro dance orchestras below the Mason and Dixon line have discouraged further trips, even though lately there has been some improvement over the barrage of Coca-Cola bottles which once greeted Cab Calloway. Segregation policies of the South create hardships on such bands which are more irksome than the amount of money involved, especially since Canada, without any discrimination, offers as good a financial turn-out. And while on the subject of popular Negro entertainment, it is interesting to note the exclusion policies of radio sponsors, no doubt based on the fear that those in the South who buy their products might otherwise be offended.

The orchestra of Duke Ellington has had more influence on popular music and jazz than any other group, not excepting Paul Whiteman. From its inception, roughly twenty years ago, to the present day, that influence has never once waned. Yet Mr. Ellington has never had a commercial radio program save when the United States Treasury used him in weekly broadcasts to stimulate the sale of war bonds. Had Duke Ellington been white, would this have been true?

Much the same has been the experience of all Negro artists who do not follow the accepted stereotype. Guest appearances, yes, and even occasionally minor spots, such as the talented Thelma Carpenter fills on the Eddie Cantor show; but never star billing. Yet the stereotyped comedian is always in demand. The movies are equally at fault and of course prejudice is the reason. As a result the old pattern is reinforced and really worthwhile artistic expression is denied the American public.

For years what Negro intellectuals had to say was for the most part denied white America except through the printed word. There were Negro teachers who had significant contributions for American students, yet save for an occasional visiting lecture their student contacts were almost entirely limited to Negro colleges. More recently there has been a trend away from this narrowing influence, and it is a most healthful sign. Since 1942 more than fifty Negroes have been appointed to faculties as professors in thirty-one white institutions. But many of these appointments have been temporary in nature and they are still more the exception than the rule.

Educationally the Negro has been robbed—and robbed on all levels, from the shortened and cheapened jim crow elementary schools in the South* to a quota system in the North which is denied publicly, but nonetheless exists. That this is also costly to whites was recently shown in New York City.

The New York *Times* of February 23 broke a story about bias in New York institutions of higher learning. It had all the elements of dynamite. Two years before Mayor LaGuardia had appointed a fifteen-man commission, un-

---

* It has been estimated that under the present rate of progress it will take two hundred years to bring Negro educational facilities in the South up to the white levels.

der the chairmanship of Charles Evans Hughes, Jr., to make a study of possible discrimination in New York colleges. Under Dr. Dan W. Dodson, the executive director of the commission, a detailed report was prepared; but before it had been formally accepted by the full committee, someone from the *Times* gained access to the report and broke the story.

To many it was no news that Negroes, and even Jews, were discriminated against, but that there was also a quota system against Catholics and people of foreign extraction must have come as a decided shock. The unidentified dean of an unnamed medical school, for example, was quoted unofficially as saying that his school accepted no Italian-Americans because they did not make the kind of graduates in which his school could take pride.

Boiled down, the report had this to say. Discrimination against Jews, Catholics and Negroes is practiced in most private, non-sectarian schools of higher learning, and in the last decade the situation has rapidly deteriorated. Almost without exception the non-sectarian private colleges and professional schools have established limitations on students admitted from the city in all, or many, of their divisions. At the same time out-of-town institutions accept very few New Yorkers on the ground that they must give priority to their local populations. As a result all New Yorkers, but in particular Jews, Catholics and Negroes, find themselves discriminated against both in city and out-of-town institutions. Actually the state of New York ranks *lowest* in the United States in its support of higher education.

This situation is not new nor is it limited to New York.

# THE HIGH COST OF PREJUDICE

The quota system is fairly universal in America, usually with the justification that without such restrictions the school would become largely a Jewish, Negro or Catholic university. The answer, of course, is that if only one institution were to lower the bars this might be true, for the same reason that when the black ghetto cracks at one point there is a concentrated flood through that breach. But if all institutions abolished quotas it is quite evident that there would not be enough Jews, Negroes and Catholics to accomplish this domination, since not all of them would want to go to the same college. Actually all institutions of higher learning do not have quotas. State universities usually do not, for example, and there are other exceptions, but by and large this number is very small.

There are some interesting costs involved in the quota set-up, and one of the most costly seems to be its effect on the potential available for creating doctors in the United States. True, under normal conditions we always seemed to have enough doctors to keep us healthy, but as a result of the war we find ourselves in the reverse position. Nor is it likely that this will change in the near future. Dr. Harold Diehl, of the University of Minnesota Medical School, estimates that by 1948 there will be only two thousand premedical students eligible for entrance into our schools of medicine. This is only one-third the normal freshman enrollment.

Of course it is senseless to blame this all on prejudice and discrimination. The refusal of selective service authorities to defer medical students is largely responsible, but certainly bias has played its part. Another sidelight is a case of what *might* have happened, dangerous conjecture perhaps, but nonetheless revealing. The whole blood plasma set-up which was so instrumental in keeping down our war casualties, was the result of research done by Dr. Charles S. Drew, who happens to be a Negro. If Drew had been unable to get into medical school, as many Negroes are, or if he had lived in the South where he would have been denied the research facilities necessary to making the blood bank a reality, we would have suffered a real loss. It is, of course, possible that another doctor might have accomplished the same results, but how many lives might have been lost in the meantime?

To leave the realm of conjecture and get back to actual facts, one aspect of the Dodson report is clearly indicative of the high cost of prejudice—the recommendation that a state university be created as a means of combating this academic bias. It is quite true that New York has no state university, and the need for one may be perfectly legitimate; yet the launching of such a project merely to fight bias and discrimination seems the costliest kind of folly. For one thing, although the Dodson report suggests $50,000,000 as the initial cost, Dr. William J. Wallin, chancellor of the state board of regents, estimates that an adequate institution would mean a capital outlay of $414,-000,000 and an annual upkeep in the neighborhood of $90,000,000.

Even if we overlook this cost it is not at all certain that such an institution might not set a dangerous pattern. Releasing the quota system only at one point usually means that all those shut off from normal entry, concentrate at that point. It results in a different kind of ghetto, but a ghetto nevertheless. One such example is Howard University, now one of the largest Negro* colleges in the country, but once an institution open to any student regardless of race, creed or color. This does not mean by inference that a state university in New York would turn into a Negro college, but one result would be that those private institutions which already had quotas would intensify their discrimination and possibly even lower existing quotas. Minorities of all kinds would concentrate into the proposed state school.

If, on purely academic grounds, there is real need for a state university, New York should certainly establish such an institution. But it should not be established solely for the purpose of fighting bias. At least, before its doors were opened, the existing discrimination among private institutions should be abolished once and for all. One way of doing this would be to shut off all public grants and tax exemptions from such colleges until they clean house. Another would be to broaden the powers of the State Commission Against Discrimination so that it could force such action, something it cannot do under its existing charter in fields other than business. Both are legislative problems. Which is more practical should be the concern of the state legislature. But the one thing least needed is another costly and duplicating investigation. The facts are already known. No community, large or small, can afford to waste any of the human resources at its command.

---

* There are still a few whites attending Howard, mainly in the graduate schools.

---

110

## CHAPTER ELEVEN

## THE PREJUDICES OF THOSE PREJUDICED AGAINST

ONE OF the least likely places to find prejudice should be among minority groups, yet this is far from true. One reason for this is that the mores of a society reach all levels of that society, and prejudice is an infectious disease. Scapegoating is only the quite natural urge to blame your troubles on someone else. But such prejudices weaken the fight against bias all along the line, splitting up what might otherwise be a solid front of minority pressure. But because both the extent and the intent of such prejudice is often misunderstood, it is worth looking into more carefully. The probable core of much of this prejudice is simply class feeling, the same sort of class snobbery which exists in the majority group. The Negro stereotype has made us lose sight of the obvious fact that there are well defined class lines in the Negro community, and they are as closely drawn as in any other society. If such class snobbery seems ridiculous to us, let us remember that it is patterned after our own.

The Negro, after all, has been in America for over three hundred years and there are old families in that group, just as there are old families among Anglo-Saxon Americans. Many of them place great emphasis on the fact that they spring from free, rather than slave forebears; and they

111

are likely to be as snobbish about it as white Americans whose ancestors came over on the Mayflower. If this seems foolish it is no more so among Negroes than among whites. Yet most whites are at a complete loss to break away from the familiar stereotype, as was shown at one of the Balls held in Washington to celebrate the birthday of Franklin Delano Roosevelt several years ago.

Since Washington is a jim crow town, a separate gathering was held by Negro society. The purpose of these dances is to raise money for the National Infantile Paralysis Foundation, and a well-meaning but empty-headed white actress from Hollywood agreed to make a guest appearance as an added attraction. Hoping to establish some sort of rapprochement with her well-to-do and socially prominent audience, she said: "I bring you greetings from my maid Beulah."

The coldness with which this remark was received and the lack of applause that her act was accorded, were things she in no way understood. Yet had she made the same remark before a white audience of the same social stratum, her reception would have been equally frigid and she would have known the reason. The sad truth is that few white Americans are capable of understanding that all Negroes are not pullman porters or domestic servants.

The attitudes some Negroes show toward other Negroes from the West Indies is often made much of by those who are quick to point out prejudices among Negroes. It exists and it is lamentable, but it is disappearing. Of all Negro prejudices this is perhaps the most easily understood, for it is a clear case of the scapegoating which appears in all minority groups. Differences in language, customs and dress are always an easy target, not only for the majority but for the minority. Basically it is the feeling that those who follow the cultural norm of the majority are more American than newcomers who have not yet reached that status.

What is intended here is not an apology for such prejudices, but an attempt to show them in their proper perspective. They, like all prejudices, are costly to those who practice them, but they are on the decrease rather than the increase.

Color, or rather the lack of it, has been of great importance in Negro life in America. Although this is less true today, it still has certain advantages which cannot be overlooked if we want to understand the way in which such feelings have come into being. In the past, fair Negroes have often found it easier to get jobs—and jobs which carry a certain status, both without and within the community. Not that such individuals were more intelligent. They merely had a lower visibility point; they merged in more readily with the dominant norm. In other cases they have even found it more to their advantage to "pass," that is, pass over into the white group and live as whites. There are a great many cases of this, probably far more than we whites are conscious of. Some of those who passed went all the way, cutting off from their former way of life and contacts entirely. Others merely did so for the sake of jobs, returning to the Negro community at night and living as they had always lived.

# THE HIGH COST OF PREJUDICE

Actually, from a purely technical standpoint and entirely from the Southern point of view, one of the worst blunders that the South made was in not exploiting the breach which it had created between light and dark Negroes. There was a time in our not too distant past, for example, when the census was taken in parts of the South on the basis of white, colored and Negro. There was also a favored position for individuals of mixed blood, less so than whites but nonetheless easier than the status of full Negro. But the South's insistence that one drop of colored blood made anyone a Negro, brought about by the new black codes put into effect after the defeat of Reconstruction, started a process which was to eventually weld all Negroes together into one great protest group.

The original breach probably goes back even farther and its origin is to be found in the different status of field-hand and house servant during slavery. House servants were more likely to have an admixture of white blood, easier work and privileges not granted those who worked in the fields, and closer ties with their white masters. One proof of this is the fact that a large percentage of the more than two hundred recorded slave revolts were betrayed by Negro house servants.

Even after slavery was abolished by law these ties between servants and the owners of the houses in which they had worked remained intact. In fact in many ways they became even closer. Right up to the point where the white aristocracy lost political control in the post-bellum period it was well aware that one of the most effective wedges it had against the poor white was the light Negro. Actually such Negroes had more in common with upper-class whites than with poor whites, a situation that the aristocracy had carefully cultivated for political reasons. That darker Negroes resented this and did not wholly trust this relationship seems quite natural.

The poor whites fell easily into this trap. They hated slavery because it was unfair competition in a system which drove them into the ground economically. Let anyone who doubts this read *The Impending Crisis* by Hinton Helper, one of the most effective ante-bellum attacks on slavery ever put to paper. Helper, a poor white from the South, hated slavery with a bitterness unrivaled by the most rabid abolitionist; yet he was led into the common error of hating the Negro with the same bitterness, because he confused the effect with the cause.

If there was a secondary caste system among Negroes at one time in our history, it was a part of the larger caste system; and it functioned with the full approval of the ruling class of the South. And even in the North there was a time when a light-colored man or woman could get ahead faster because of the misguided conceit of whites, who assumed that merely because of an admixture of white blood such individuals were more intelligent. This was pure nonsense, yet it is probable that even some Negroes believed this, particularly those with light complexions.

There have been numerous examples of counter-movements set up in opposition to this caste within a caste. Marcus Garvey, who extolled all that was black and gave to the Negro masses its first real ego build-up, was not only intensely anti-white but also violently anti-mulatto

Many Negroes realize the dangers in such extreme

"nationalism" as Garvey advocated, and today the antagonism between light and dark Negroes, though it has not entirely disappeared, has reached a point where, aside from social snobbery, it has no real importance. It has been replaced by a solidarity which exerts one of the strongest pressures toward the breakdown of the discrimination pattern.

It has been said that anti-Semitism among Negroes is widespread, but it has also been claimed to be non-existent. Actually the truth lies somewhere between those two extremes, exactly where is hard to say; but the incidence is likely to be basically the same as among Americans as a whole, though of fairly recent advent.

During the last depression a number of violent anti-Semites turned up in Negro communities. An example is Sufi Abdul Hamid, the black Hitler of Harlem, whose tall, fancy-draped figure was familiar on many uptown street corners. There were also a number of cults whose followers took Moorish names and seemed more interested in the words of the Koran than those of the Bible. Not to be ignored were the short-lived hate sheets, *Dynamite* and *Negro Youth*, both definitely anti-Semitic in character. However, one should remember that such manifestations were as familiar in the white community.

Another factor which is not always understood is that part of what seems on the surface anti-Semitism is actually a misdirected anti-white feeling. Actually true anti-Semitism is a more or less new phenomenon in Negro life and largely limited to urban centers. In the geographic sense, it is Northern rather than Southern. Its roots are to be found in the fact that white landlords, merchants and employers have exploited Negroes in every large urban segregated area. Negroes usually pay ten to fifteen per cent more in rents when they move into a neighborhood, and it has been estimated that most Negroes pay $1.15 to get $1.00 worth of groceries.

It does not matter that all the stores around a community, all the apartments and all the employers, do not happen to be Jewish. *Some* are. And the American mores have taught *some* Negroes to use Jews as scapegoats to hit back against this exploitation. Agitators have been quick to argue that all landlords, merchants and employers around the fringes of the ghetto are Jews, and the lesson has been learned to the extent that even an Irish store may be called by some a jewstore. Gentile apartment owners, store proprietors and employers have been guilty of rent gouging, markups and peon wages and so have some Jews. Yet the blame has been falling on the head of the Jew in the Negro community of late, just as it has in America at large.

A case in point was the so-called slave marts of the depression. Negro women gathered at designated spots where white housewives hired them by the hour at rates which varied between ten and twenty-five cents. The spots which received the most publicity happened to be in the Bronx, a Jewish community for the most part; but non-Jewish housewives were just as guilty of the practice, in New York and elsewhere. Such goings-on were vicious and there is no justification for their existence. But Jews

117

got all the blame and the memory is still bitterly ingrained in many Negro women who work as domestics.

But it is not true that anti-Semitism, or its counterpart, anti-Negro feelings among Jews, is either as disrupting or as widespread as many people claim. True, there are Negroes who are and will no doubt continue to be anti-Semitic, just as some Jews will continue to look upon Negroes as inferior. Both help reinforce the prejudice and discrimination which hurts both. The leaders of both groups, however, are well aware of the dangers involved and have worked hard for a rapprochement between the two minorities. There has always been a core in existence. The Julius Rosenwald Fund has done a great deal for Negro education in the South, and it awards its fellowship grants without thought to the race, creed or color of the applicant. And there were Jews among the founders of both the National Association for the Advancement of Colored People and the National Urban League.

The issues involved have received frank discussion in periodicals sponsored by both groups. One of the main differences, as Dr. L. D. Reddick, curator of the Schomberg Collection and a firm advocate of collective action, has pointed out, is that Jews in the United States are fighting to *maintain* their rights, while Negroes are fighting to *win* theirs. Some Jews feel that as a result the two struggles are on different levels and naturally conflicting. Yet all Jews do not feel this way by any manner of means. To most it is becoming more and more apparent that any split among minorities plays right into the hands of those who hope to continue to exploit and discriminate against all minorities. It is the old "divide and conquer" tactic.

Certainly Negroes have reason to hate whites and a great many do. The feeling ranges all the way from bitterness with homicidal overtones, down to the folklore level of devastatingly satirical stories about the doings of Miss Ann and Mr. Charley. One of the main difficulties, as Horace Cayton* has pointed out, is that in their relationship with whites Negroes are not only unsure why they are being punished, but equally uncertain why they are often praised. What may be the accepted racial etiquette in one situation may turn out to be a racial insult in another; the ways of Jacksonville may not be the ways of Memphis or Dallas. As a result many Negroes live in a psychiatric maze of confused symbols, forced each day to go through a series of psychological lynchings. They are never sure what will happen when they go into a restaurant or try to shop in a store. Is the unfortunate happening that results merely a normal complication or the expected racial slur? They can never be sure. It makes many Negroes draw within themselves and avoid contacts with whites—a form of self-segregation. Often such individuals take on attitudes of intense race-consciousness and acquire a blustering hostility toward all whites.

This has often brought them into open conflict with the Southern white's conception of the "good Negro" and his

---

* *Black Metropolis* by Horace R. Cayton and St. Clair Drake. Harcourt, Brace.

white folks, the patronizing and idyllic fable which was once partial fact. Even in the South there has been an increased militancy among younger Negroes, which is usually in direct opposition to the policy of close coopera· tion with whites which was advocated by Booker T. Washington. Older and more conservative Negroes still cling to the old ways, but the pressures against them have reached proportions which threaten to sweep them aside. For one thing the drive to maintain the status quo has tended to make even the "good" white folks ineffectual. The progress of Negro gains in the South has been more than matched by an improvement in the lot of the average white Southerner. Using this as a measuring stick, Negroes in the South are still not much better off than they have always been.

Out of this ideological struggle have come symbols which complicate the already complex, tragi-comic relationship between whites and Negroes. The most significant of these is the "race hero," a direct result of our own prejudices. He appears on many levels, but his rôle is always to fight back against white oppression. He may be the Negro who, guilty or innocent, goes to the electric chair without once cracking under the strain or showing his fear to the white folks. Again he may be the one lone Negro facing a white mob who says, in effect, *Maybe they will kill me, but when I go I'm taking a couple of these white folks along with me.*

He has been put to paper by a powerful young novelist*

---

* *If He Hollers Let Him Go* by Chester B. Himes. Doubleday.

in the character of Bob Jones, a Negro who comes to the West Coast from the Middle West to work in a shipyard during the war. A product of the effects of racial tensions and the frustrations inherent in our culture, he has turned into a mechanism that reacts by hitting out blindly. To give up means that he will go down, become the thing he hates and fears most. Above all he is filled with contempt for the Negro who gives in and plays the white folks' game. He wants a normal life, but he knows that he can eventually have one only by somehow resolving things by violence. At the same time he both fears and hates violence. He is an animal in a steel trap.

The "race hero" usually raises antagonism among most whites with whom he has any contact. Just as most reviewers missed the whole point of Himes's book, so do most whites fail to see what their own actions have been doing over a number of years. What we think brash is very often the result of real courage, and if we do not like it we shall have to modify the attitudes which produce such actions. Otherwise it will become more and more impossible for Negroes and whites to have normal relations.

So long as our mores demand that we judge all Negroes as Negroes, the same must of necessity be true of the Negro's reactions toward us. Whatever a Negro does, we judge him by this inflexible standard. If we are prejudiced, we say he did such-and-such a thing because of his racial traits. If we are not, we usually say he did it because of the way we have treated him. That he may be merely a good or a bad human being never seems to enter our mind, nor can it under our present attitudes.

121

# THE HIGH COST OF PREJUDICE

This is not the basis for either intelligent judgment or a decent relationship between individuals or groups. White stereotypes are created as readily as Negro stereotypes. There are good and bad individuals in every stratum of society, and Negroes are no exception to the rule. Yet under our existing mores, personality counts for little in Negro-white relationships. And here we have one of the main blocks to racial peace in America.

## CHAPTER TWELVE

## HOLD THAT LINE!

THE NEGRO is in danger of becoming lost in a maze of statistics, graphs and charts. He has been surveyed and investigated to death by sociologists, anthropologists, psychiatrists, psychologists and experts in the field of race relations. The results have in turn been boiled down by writers and presented to the layman in capsule form. In all, social-minded organizations have probably spent enough money on race relations in the last twenty-five years to clean up every Negro slum in the United States.

By now it would seem that we should know what the Negro problem is. If we don't, according to A. Clayton Powell, Sr.,* any ten-year-old black boy on the street corner of any racial ghetto can tell us, and in terms that are more easily understood than those used by the experts. In fact "race relations," possibly without realizing it, has become a respectable upholder of the status quo, instead of the radical gadfly it was originally. It has been preaching tolerance, when tolerance is no longer enough.

The number of organizations which now devote their full time to race relations must be staggering. They overlap badly, and as a result much of their effectiveness is dissipated. Too often their appeal is mainly directed toward those who are already convinced. On a dollars-and-

* *Riots and Ruin* by A. Clayton Powell. Robert W. Smith.

cents basis, in relation to the numbers affected, they are for the most part inefficient. This is not suggested as a plea for abolishing race-relations work, but rather for a consolidation and realigning of sights.

Horace Cayton, the Chicago sociologist, makes an apt comparison to witch doctors and conjure men, practitioners of mumbo-jumbo in a tribal society. In our quest for a solution of the so-called Negro problem we resemble an ignorant man looking for a patent medicine. He hates to spend the extra money. He knows that he aches, and the posters on the back of the medicine wagon fascinate him; though he knows there is a good doctor around the corner. Good for man or beast, the sign says. Cures anything. Fine for pregnant mothers. Harmless to even a tiny child.

The whole history of our recent race-relations work is that we have tried to work out a solution within the framework of the status quo. In fact this is pretty much true of our whole history in relationship to the Negro. After the Civil War Negroes merely exchanged the status of chattel slavery for economic bondage, as anyone can see who cares to look up the facts on peonage in the South over the last half century. The "Separate but Equal" ideal, as we have seen, proves to be *separate and unequal*. In fact the gradualism of the Southern white liberal has proven so gradual that it could hardly keep up with itself. One suspects that, in the North and South alike, an overdose of race relations has tended to reinforce the way things are rather than make them the way they should be.

Whites have not been the only offenders in this respect. Negroes who have tended to slow up progress have not usually done so purposely, in spite of the fact that many of them have a vested interest in segregation. There is nothing wrong in trying to maintain racial harmony; racial tensions are nasty and destructive forces and they set up dangerous currents which affect us all. They should by all means be kept at a minimum, but not at the expense of normal progress toward a lasting solution. Too often whites and Negroes have done this very thing, because they did not realize how dangerous such a course could be in freezing the status quo.

The name of Booker T. Washington comes at once to mind. Though Mr. Washington has been dead for a long time, his shadow still hangs over the South. But it is easier to deflate the policies of the man than it is to debunk the man himself, though in recent years a number of attempts have been made. That Mr. Washington was sincere is not open to question, nor is the fact that, right or wrong, he accomplished great things. He provided leadership when it was most needed, and improved race relations in the South. To a degree he also improved the lot of the average Negro in the South.

And yet, in spite of this, he also gave to the white South a potent weapon for freezing the status quo, one which has survived to this day. His policies are still the policies of most white liberals in the South, whose only program for progress stays within the permanent limits of segregation. Mr. Washington also pioneered a technique for attaining leadership which has been used by many Negroes with neither his ability nor his sincerity.

Moreover the Negro colleges of the South have been mainly patterned on the model of Washington's Tuskegee, an industrial and manual-training school which prepared Negroes for the only jobs available to them at that time, in order that they might gain economic stability. In this Washington had the full support of the white South, which was perfectly willing to have better trained and more reliable servants, waiters, handymen, tenant farmers and unskilled workers so long as they remained "good" Negroes and had no uppity ideas. And the same is true today.

For the white South has never been able to visualize a Negro college which produced educated Negroes, or the need of modifying the mores of the region to absorb even a small number of such graduates when they did mysteriously appear. Too much education was thought of as harmful for most Negroes—and apparently still is, to quote the Texas legislator who was faced with a bill to provide for an institution to train Negro lawyers in his own state. "I'm a lawyer myself," he said, "and I could take one law book and teach all the 'niggers' in this state all the law they need to know in six months."

But in addition to the shadow of Booker T. Washington there is another factor to be considered, the hangover from the missionary societies which founded and still support so many Negro colleges in the South. After the cessful termination of the Civil War the North awoke suddenly to the realization that it was up to them to do something about the Negroes they had fought so hard to free from slavery. Reconstruction and the Freedman's Bureau were partial answers, but only temporary ones. The missionaries, who had earlier advocated colonization and were the main force behind the experiment in Liberia hoped to find the answer in education. Just what this educational process was in preparation for, remains in doubt; but it may have been they hoped to train a better type of colonist, who would in turn spread Christianity to the natives of the land where he was set. Whatever the reason for this educational program, however, there seems to have been more emphasis on cold showers in the morning and prayers at night than on the liberal arts and sciences. But more important, such colleges have helped to perpetuate the tradition of a separate culture and economy within the rigid bounds of segregation. For the most part they continue to do so today.

There was a day when all such colleges were headed by white missionaries, but that day is nearly past. It has given way to the Negro president and administration, though usually the actual control remains largely in the hands of white trustees. In most cases the new presidents have come either directly from the ranks of the ministry, or at best one generation removed. This pattern has been almost as pronounced among state-controlled and even privately endowed institutions. One suspects that the main reason for this has been that with such men there is a better than even chance that the status quo will be rigidly maintained.

Such reasoning is not to be taken as an attack upon the Protestant or any other church, certainly not against Christianity. But it seems no more logical that a man trained for the ministry should of necessity make the best college president than that a well-trained academician would make the best pastor of a large church. And if the church in the South is often a rigid barricade against breaking the status quo of segregation, it can only be judged as going contrary to Christ's ideas of the brother-hood of man.

The effects of these hangovers have been widespread. Although many Negro colleges have broken fundamentally with the educational policies of Booker T. Washington and revamped their curricula along strictly liberal-arts lines, they have often been hampered by what could aptly be called absentee control. The argument for this caution is usually that the student body is drawn from the South and students should be trained to get along under the mores of the region where they will live. Two factors, however, limit the effectiveness of this argument. One is that Negro colleges in the South are drawing more and more students from the North, either because parents cannot afford the colleges in their area or, because of the quota system, have difficulty in getting their children accepted. The second is that the best trained and qualified graduates are likely to go North where better job opportunities exist.

This is not to imply that Negro colleges in the South, or in the North for that matter, are not competent institutions. There are many with up-to-date plants, qualified faculties and high academic standards. Yet too often faculty salaries are low, and departments are handicapped by inadequate personnel. There have also been instances where administration officials have hampered academic projects they considered dangerously radical, measured against the status quo.

Too often we fail to understand that segregation has sometimes made it possible for some Negroes to gain an unfair advantage because we have placed them in jobs they could not hope to gain under normal competition. From maudlin sentimentality and the hope of relieving our guilt-feelings, we have allowed some Negroes to go to the top the easy way and without the proper qualifications. We forget this, because they are willing to retain the status quo—almost as willing as we are. Many have made a career of what Negroes cynically refer to as "fooling the white folks" and the returns have been considerable, both in terms of money and of prestige. The phrase is more apt than many of us realize.

The whole process was summed up by a visitor to Tuskegee Institute. He was standing beside a large statue of Booker T. Washington on the campus. The statue is a rather prominent and well executed piece of bronze, showing a crouched Negro under a multi-folding covering which Mr. Washington is in the act of lifting. After looking at the work for a few moments the visitor said:

"You know for the life of me I can't figure out whether Booker T. is lifting the veil of ignorance from the Negro's brow or hiding him from the white folks."

The church in the South has been doing some recent thinking on the Negro, as a report* by the chairman of the Commission on the American Baptist Theological Seminary shows. It is one of the clearest expressions of the grass-roots racial attitudes of the white South to appear in some time. The pattern is familiar, yet there is a new alertness to the gravity of the situation and even a slight

* "The New Racial Situation—The Way Out" by E. P. Alldredge. *The Quarterly Review*, a Survey of Southern Baptist Progress.

inclination to retreat a little—but always within the rigid pattern of segregation. Yet at the same time there is complete lack of understanding of the relationship of basic problems to the economy of the South.

The report discusses the pros and cons of three methods of solution of the Negro problem—colonization, integration and Christianization. The last of these is merely another name for the equitable distribution and administration of the familiar policy of "Separate but Equal." As one would expect, the author advocates No. 1 or No. 3, and rules No. 2 out completely. The interesting thing is the impracticability of both solutions advocated, and a total blindness to the staggering costs involved.

It is unnecessary to go into the policy of colonization except to say that it was once strongly advocated by Thomas Jefferson and Abraham Lincoln; but at the present time its one vocal champion is Theodore "The Man" Bilbo. The one real trial of this system, the experiment in Liberia, has proven unsuccessful, and there seems little hope that future attempts would prove otherwise. Yet Mr. Alldredge claims: "granting that a proper territory can be found, colonization is the simplest and easiest way out of a very difficult and dangerous situation which is growing more perilous every year."

Actually how simple and easy would it be? According to the report, "the only serious question about colonization is the finding of a territory suitable for the settlement and future welfare of 13,000,000 Negroes." Even the initial cost of such a territory is by no means the only expense as Mr. Alldredge notes, for such a policy would also call for the reimbursement to Negroes for all their personal losses, assisting them to establish new homes, schools and churches in their new state, and subsidizing their government and its industries for a period of from twelve to twenty years.

This writer does not know the "going" price on a property as large as Arkansas, Kansas, Missouri and Oklahoma combined, nor the amount of property reimbursement and subsidization necessary to float such a project, but it is bound to be more than we ought to have to pay for our prejudices. And since two-third of the Negroes to be exported live in the South, which accordingly should bear two-thirds of the financial burden, what would happen to the already inadequate Southern economy?

Something more basic is involved, however, and the report overlooks it completely. Even if such a policy were fair to both races, which obviously it isn't, how could it be set in motion? Certainly not by a two-thirds majority in either House, or by a ratification by two-thirds of the states. A national referendum seems just as doubtful, if we assume that, since Negroes have been here for over three hundred years, they have a right to vote on such a question. If we are on the conservative side and estimate that only ten million Negroes vote against such a project, and every white in the South voted for it—if only half of the North voted, and half of that half voted against it— there would still not be the necessary majority.

Colonization is, of course, pure nonsense and stands no chance of even serious consideration. Even in the South it seems extremely doubtful that more than two-thirds of the people would agree to such an obvious denial of civil rights. The cost angle alone would probably make the

South hesitate before committing financial suicide, no matter how deeply ingrained its prejudices.

We have already seen that the same applies to an equal administration of "Separate but Equal." Thus it seems apparent that the grass-roots South is basically interested in holding the line, in spite of its cry that it is sincere in wanting a solution.

Most typical of the interracial organizations which are unconsciously holding the line for the status quo is the Southern Regional Council, which grew out of two parent movements—the Commission on Interracial Cooperation, founded in 1919, and the Durham-Atlanta-Richmond conferences of 1942–43. Again one finds it difficult to condemn a group of sincere men whose motives are of the best, but whose personalities are somewhat confused because they are publicly advocating a policy which privately a majority of them do not condone. That policy is segregation.

On October 20, 1942, a group of Southern Negroes met in Durham, North Carolina. Emphasizing their Southernness—and their purpose, as the changes which in their opinion would benefit not only Negroes but whites—a statement was issued which supposedly embodied the thinking of the conference. That there was nothing new in the statement should have surprised no one, for the Negro, North and South, had been saying the same thing for years. But the statement was couched in forthright language, with the possible exception of the brief section dealing with segregation.

It reads: "We are fundamentally opposed to the principle and practice of compulsory segregation in our American society, whether of races, of classes, or creeds; however we regard it as both sensible and timely to address ourselves now to the current problems of racial discrimination and neglect, and to ways in which we may cooperate in the advancement of programs aimed at the sound improvement of race relations within the democratic framework."

Actually the meeting was far from unanimous on this item. There were some who had felt that the "however" should have read "moreover" and a minority had strongly protested pussyfooting at all on the subject of segregation. At any rate the meeting's statement brought about a gathering of white liberals in Atlanta who felt that "the Durham statement seemed so frank and courageous, so free from any suggestion of threat and ultimatum, and at the same time shows such good will, that we gladly agree to cooperate." This meeting's counter-statement read in part: "It is futile to imagine or to assert that the problem will solve itself. The need is for a positive program arrived at in an atmosphere of understanding, cooperation and mutual respect."

Next a joint conference was called in Richmond on June 16, 1943, composed of delegates from both the Durham and the Atlanta meetings and a continuing committee was appointed to work out "methods and practical means of approach." The result was the Southern Regional Council which took over the existing facilities of the Commission on Interracial Cooperation on February 16, 1944.

Two facts seem fairly obvious. The first is that any sort of concrete action was approximately fourteen months in gestation. The other is that the final result, SRC, was at least in part a duplication of an interracial group already long in existence. Nothing which has happened since in any way causes this writer to modify that statement or to feel that Lillian Smith, herself a Southerner, was wrong in suggesting that they were less interested in attaining human equality for the Negro than in assuring a better reputation for the Southern white man.

The work of the SRC has not been meaningless. Short of publicly disavowing segregation it has said all the right things, endorsed all the worthy causes and issued more of the same literature which a network of similar organizations, North and South, have been distributing for years. It has stated that it is working on a series of surveys. But we have already said that further investigations of something already known is merely another delaying action. It is interesting to note that, because of the Council's refusal to face the question of segregation squarely, at least three officers have resigned from the organization, two of them white, the third a Negro.

The Southern Regional Council is not the only one guilty of the stalling tactics which are helping to hold the line. Organizations, both in the South and North, are guilty of the same thing in a variety of ways. They are playing inter-organization politics, appointing self-perpetuating officers and becoming as ingrown as the most exclusive gentleman's club. In the meantime time is running out.

## CHAPTER THIRTEEN

## HOW LIBERAL IS A LIBERAL?

VIEWING THE racial picture objectively, it seems we have overlooked one basic fact—just exactly what it is that we are trying to accomplish. No other assumption is possible save for the very cynical thought that perhaps we do not really want to solve the Negro problem. If we rule out this, just what is it that the Negro wants and we seem so loath to give him, though not doing so may drive us into financial and moral bankruptcy?

If we did not already know, a Southern university press* in 1944 published the answer in a symposium by fourteen representative Negroes. By vocation eight were educators, three labor leaders, two writers and one the Assistant Executive Secretary of the National Association for the Advancement of Colored People. Politically five might be called radical, five liberal and four conservative. The only stipulation made by the publisher was that equal representation be given to every shade of political thought and that no contributor go to extremes which he could not justify. Although the reader was asked to draw his own conclusions, a lengthy introduction by a self-avowed Southern liberal, W. T. Couch, at that time editor-in-chief

---

* *What the Negro Wants.* Edited by Rayford W. Logan. Chapel Hill.

of the University of North Carolina Press, made it quite clear that the publishers were disappointed with the results. They disagreed with most of the opinions expressed, and even claimed that the whole approach of the social sciences was based on a false premise.

What was this heresy which appeared in all the essays? Simply stated, it was the fact that Negroes merely wanted to be treated as first-class citizens in a country where they had lived for three hundred years and thought of as their native land. Since they were Americans and not Africans, they had no desire for a shiny new colony off somewhere in the distance. They just wanted the same chance to prove or disprove themselves that any other citizen enjoyed, no more, no less. As Americans they wanted no special privileges, nor any discriminations because their skin happened to be darker than that of their fellow-citizens. But what seemed to particularly harass Mr. Couch was that, Northern or Southern—radical, liberal or conservative—none of the fourteen saw any way of accomplishing this without first doing away with segregation.

It is difficult to see how any intelligent person who weighs all the factors in the Southern economy against any possible solution through a policy of honestly administered "Separate but Equal" could arrive at any other realistic conclusion. Only if we want to perpetuate the Negro problem can we fail to realize this simple fact. True, we can go on *slowly* improving the lot of the Negro at the same time we are *rapidly* bettering our own. We can build more Negro colleges and more heavily endow those already in existence, in order to educate more and more Negroes for jobs which do not and never will exist for them under the status quo. We can provide token public and semi-public segregated housing to an extent which may slightly lower crime and disease statistics. But, so long as there is forced segregation, black ghettoes will pyramid faster than we can renovate them. We can increase the pay for "Negro" jobs in good times, and raise relief allotments in bad times; but without going bankrupt we can never gain anything by these measures save temporary objectives. We can decry militancy among Negroes, saying that without cooperation no progress is possible; yet, so long as Negroes are forced to remain second- or third-class citizens, we will only produce more frustrations, whose only release is open hostility. It may even be possible to control racial tensions at a point short of actual violence, but we will still have a Negro problem.

The problem of race is not a Southern problem alone. With the migrations to the North which originated in World War I it became a national problem, and with the technological advances of World War II, which visibly compressed the size of the globe, it has taken on the aspect of a world problem. The fact nonetheless remains that, until the mores of the South are radicaly modified, it will be a Southern problem in the sense that one key log always causes a jam, regardless of how much may be piled up in back of it.

What is it that the white South fears? What is the nature of a psychosis so deeply ingrained that it makes men cling to a way of life which keeps them not only ignorant but poor as well? Or as Howard Odum, the Southern sociologist puts it, what is it that makes good men in the South do bad things—to which we might add, makes liberals afraid to be liberal and speak out in public against that which they privately decry? Noting the injustice of quoting a statement out of its context and making due allowances for Southern oratory, how could a man* who calls himself a Southern liberal say: "There is no power in the world—not even in all the mechanized armies of the earth, Allied and Axis—which could now force the Southern white people into the abandonment of the principle of social segregation."

We will not find the answer in the mouths of the Southern liberals or in the rantings of the bigots and racists. It is in the heart of the grass-roots, where a whole layer of fairly decent and humane people react to what they hear and what they are told. The bugaboo of a mulatto America has always been high on the list of techniques for maintaining a complete separation of the races. To return to Mr. Alldredge † and his report to the Southern Baptists, we find the statement that if segregation were abolished in the South only one race would be left, a mulatto race having from "one-tenth to two-tenths Negro blood." Yet in the North, where there is little if any legal segregation, this has not happened; nor in those states which allow mixed marriages, have such unions increased to a point likely to produce such results, even taking into consideration the smaller Negro-to-white ratio in those areas. The plain

---

* Mark Ethridge, Editor of the Louisville *Courier-Journal*.
† "The New Racial Situation—The Way Out" by E. P. Alldredge. *The Quarterly Review*, a Survey of Southern Baptist Progress.

truth is that people do not marry because of segregation or the lack of it, nor has jim crow ever prevented miscegenation.

Actually it is estimated that less than a fourth of American Negroes do not have some white blood, a condition which the segregated South is possibly even more responsible for than the unsegregated North. There is also, by a queer quirk in the Southern mores, a percentage—how large or small it is difficult to say—of pure whites within the Negro group. At one time in the South, if a white woman had children by both a white and a Negro, all the children were usually classified as colored. There are also individuals within the white group who have a small admixture of Negro blood because of the phenomenon of "passing," where light Negroes have changed their names and by moving into a new area have been absorbed by the white group. This interchange has been placed as low as 15,000 annually, as high as 30,000.

In many parts of the South there is a clearly defined colored branch of white families where there will be two sets of cousins, one white and the other colored. The folk tales of New Orleans are full of such instances, and though they are often exaggerated there is a basis of fact. Until fairly recently in many parts of the South a white man might maintain two households without so much as a raised eyebrow in the community.

These factors are introduced merely to show the difficulties involved in arriving at even an approximation of how much Negro blood there might be under complete amalgamation, which is not likely to happen during our lifetime or the lifetime of our children, if at all. It has even been estimated that if Negroes were merely desirous of becoming lighter, they could eventually arrive at that state of coloration by selective interminglings within their own group. But the point is that we are not talking about guinea pigs but about human beings, and human beings have a peculiar habit of marrying persons with whom they fall in love. Until it has been established that every Negro wants to marry a white, or that every white wants to marry a Negro, the whole question of a mulatto America is in every sense a black herring dragged across the path to frighten people into thinking with their emotions.

In fact what would happen if segregation were abolished in the South overnight? No one knows, of course; but there is more than a suspicion that for half a century or more there would be very little change in a purely social sense. Southerners have made much of the voluntary segregation of the Jews. They have insisted that all they are trying to do is to allow Negroes to keep to themselves. It is true that Jews have, to a large degree, shut themselves off, but they have not had to resort to restrictive covenants, forced and legal segregation, or anti-gentile riots to do so.

Actually what these whites forget is that people are drawn together because of common interests. That core remains constant, even though some individuals may deviate from it. What whites see as the desire on the part of Negroes to be "white," is in truth an urge to attain the status which, because of our prejudices and discriminations, being "white" in America means. If this were changed, most social scientists will verify the fact that, although there might no longer be a "Negro" church, a

"Negro" society, or even a strictly "Negro" residential area, many, and probably the majority of, Negroes would wish to remain as a core on those three levels in spite of the fact that Negroes and whites mixed freely in schools, recreational centers and restaurants.

The reasons for this are the same as those which rule all society. Some Jews have married gentiles, yet the fear of America suddenly becoming Jewish has never become a reality. Some Catholics have married non-Catholics, yet the Protestant churches have not been blighted overnight as a result. Some Negroes have married whites, and in the years to come it is possible that more will do so, yet white America is getting no darker as a result.

After all marriage is a private affair. By no means all Negroes want to worship with whites, associate with whites, or even marry whites. In fact it might surprise whites to know how many Negroes dislike them and are bored in their company. There is a great deal of difference between human equality and the loosely applied term, social equality. The first does not of necessity lead to the second, though it may by mutual consent.

If Northern whites are confused about what Southern whites think the confusion appears to work both ways. For example, Mr. Alldredge tells his Southern Baptists: "It is our considered judgment that the proposed mixed racial pattern will prove objectionable to 95 per cent of the 126,000,000 white people in the nation." The report goes on to estimate that there are 13,000,000 Negroes and 3,150,000 whites against the separation of the races, or

2½ per cent, as against 122,850,000 whites, or 97½ per cent, in favor of the separation of the races.

These figures are interesting but misleading, to say the least. Using Mr. Alldredge's own figures there are eighty-five million whites living in the North, a region which is largely without legal segregation and in which many states have civil rights and anti-bias laws with real teeth in them. If ninety-seven and a half per cent of all whites believe in the separation of the races, where were they when such bills were passed and why have they not repealed them? Such statements do not make sense, save that they help to reinforce what the South would like to believe.

Yet the South is in a process of change, and there are already slight cracks in the surface which are likely to grow larger. At one extreme is the demagogic fringe and the recently revived Ku Klux Klan. In the middle is the grass-roots South—lower middle and middle class, conservative, anti-radical and even anti-intellectual—basically a decent people but one easily swayed by the spoken and written word. At the other end is the liberal, tragically split by the race question and caught between the mores on one side and the decency of humanity on the other.

We have seen what the race issue did to the two great progressive movements in the South, and now we are in the process of going through a third. It might be wise to look at the material with which we have to work. In the days when it was still possible to be classed as a liberal for merely denying the white man's sacred right to lynch, a lot of new riders got on the bandwagon. They included not ony sheep and goats but a few fossils who had been out in front of the rank and file at the turn of the century

142

but, because they had been marking time ever since, were now at the end of the parade.

Actually there were as many kinds of liberals as there were species of flora and fauna. There was the liberal who was sentimental about the Negro, because he reminded him of the better days before the defeat of the Confederacy made the cavalier only a character in *Gone With the Wind*—if indeed, as some social historians\* have intimated, he ever existed at all. Then there were other liberals who strongly advocated the education of Negroes "within reason." They hoped this would result in better servants to take care of their personal needs. There was also the liberal who spoke for the "South" in the better magazines, where one of them † wrote that "no decent white Southerner can but view the present position of the American Negro with a sore heart, a troubled conscience and a deep compassion," yet felt that to do more would upset the status quo and only result in violence harmful to the Negro. There were liberals who called themselves Agrarians, but in the words of John Andrew Rice, in a book called *I Came Out of the Eighteenth Century,* the only plowing they ever did was in the classroom and they wrote books proving that the only way forward was the way backward. Then there were "liberals" who were forced to work within the "radical" framework of the South, and "radicals" who were forced to work within the "liberal" framework of the North.

The only thing which held together this odd assortment

---

\* W. J. Cash, for example, in *The Mind of the South.* Knopf.
† *How the South Feels* by David L. Cohn. The Atlantic Monthly.

THE HIGH COST OF PREJUDICE

of men and women was the abstract "Negro," a symbol which meant many things to many people. The thing which has recently split them is the whole question of segregation. It was inevitable that such a split should come, the amazing thing was that it had been so long in fermentation. Now for the first time it may be possible to have a real meeting of Southern and Northern liberals without the specter of the Negro haunting the meeting place.

Some who had not spoken out were sincere in not doing so. They had been silent because they were afraid of doing more harm than good, of causing racial trouble. Others were sincere but timid, for this business of being a Southerner can be as complex in its own way as being a Negro or a Jew, a Communist or a Catholic. Always there was the fear of community pressures, the loss of a job or of one's prestige, the fear that going against the mores might even result in violence against themselves. There was the conditioning of the past and the lessons which had been taught so well that they often remained deep in the subconscious.

And yet there were those who did speak out. Often they were not heard, for they were still, small voices crying in the wilderness and without access to Southern newspapers or other media of expression. Even in the North the better magazines were more interested in the meaningless but finely chiseled words of the professional liberals—in the reaffirmation of the legend—than in a realistic program for a lasting solution. Such men and women came from varied backgrounds—educated and uneducated, rich and poor, influential and without influence. They were disorganized and without leadership.

In the past few years two organizations have assumed great potential significance in the South. One, the Southern Conference for Human Welfare, grew out of the report on the South delivered to President Roosevelt by the National Emergency Council in 1938. The other was the National Citizens Political Action Committee.

Of the two, the Southern Conference for Human Welfare was on firmer ground, perhaps, for no one could accuse it of being alien or run from the outside. Under the leadership of Dr. Clark Foreman it was a rallying ground for Southerners who wanted to do something about moulding a better South. That it was a Southern voice was important; that it was headed by men and women who had standing in the South was also significant.

Citizens PAC, on the other hand, was Northern-born, frankly political, left wing and of trades-union origin. It had two things, however, in its favor. Behind it was the whole broad movement of the CIO, which was bringing unionization into the South where it was most needed and in a way that was not going to allow the race issue to be used by industry as a wedge to split workers. Secondly, in its initial foray into Southern politics, it showed a great deal of political "know-how" by knocking out a handful of the demagogues who had been most active in Washington, though some of them, seeing the handwriting on the wall, had pleaded ill health and refused to contest for reelection.

Both organizations wanted a New South and were exploiting the existing cracks in the surface. But on May 9,

# THE HIGH COST OF PREJUDICE

1946, atop historic Stone Mountain near Atlanta the Ku Klux Klan, under the fiery light from five burning crosses, showed its hand in Georgia. Five hundred new members were initiated by more than seven hundred hooded Klansmen, while a thousand wives and children looked on complacently. There was no doubt where the Klan stood in relation to that fight.

We have gone through a series of primary elections in the South, where victory in the primary, thanks to the one-party system which has been one result of our prejudices, is victory in the coming election. On the surface the results seem discouraging, and already Southern newspapers have seen in this a death blow to both SCFHW and PAC and a return to the old ways of the status quo. But it is not so simple as that. For the first time Negroes voted in many white primaries, and their right to vote has been firmly established beyond possibility of change, whatever Mr. Talmadge of Georgia may say to the contrary. Moreover the issues at stake were clearly presented for the first time in many a Southern election. Southern distrust of outside interference was probably one reason why the initial round was lost. But other rounds are coming up and not all fights are lost in the first round.

## CHAPTER FOURTEEN

# A NEW SOUTH?

ALTHOUGH it is true that the racial mores of the South are one thing which helps keep the region poor, backward and ignorant, abolishing discrimination and prejudice would not assure an automatic return to a better life. Actually the basic economy of the South, which is two hundred years behind the times, has helped produce those racial attitudes and make them an integral part of a system which has reduced the South's status to that of a poor cousin, or colony, of the more affluent North. It is quite possible that without those racial attitudes to reinforce it, the ferment of social change would have long ago swept that system aside.

The South is a region of very limited local capital and an oversupply of local unskilled labor, white and colored. Absentee ownership is more the rule than the exception, and as a result profits are syphoned off and sent out of the area. Predominantly agricultural, the South imports more than it exports; and because it is rural rather than urban it is little mechanized. Its one-crop agricultural system gave birth to the tenant or sharecropper set-up which, aside from being morally wrong in terms of the 'cropper, is wasteful to the boss-man who must carry a family for twelve months when in reality he needs their labor for at most ten weeks of each year. Granted that the outlay to

147

provide a diet of grits and side meat, an occasional pair of overalls, and a shack which could pass no reasonable health standard is small, the fact remains that even with rank exploitation it is still an uneconomic transaction.

Nor does it stop there. Two sharp critics * have extended the use of the word sharecropper to include non-farm workers in the South, because the phrase "my workers" may be heard in factory or downtown office building as readily as at the end of the cotton row. In order to maintain the system it has been necessary to make "niggers" out of Negroes and "peckerwoods" out of free farmers. Moreover in a sense it has made a slave out of anyone who works for anybody else in the South.

A region which has existed for so many years under an economy which can only function on an oversupply of cheap, docile and unskilled labor has assumed a culture peculiar to itself. It is not accidental that the Bible Belt is to be found in Dixie, or that the basic sermon preached is that man must labor hard and without protest in order to be eligible to pass through the gates of heaven. Nor is it mere chance that all labor unions should be looked upon as instruments of the devil, and the Negro must be kept in his place.

Cotton is the personification of that system. It became the main money crop of the South after the invention of the cotton gin made its production profitable, though only under chattel slavery or its successor, peonage or economic bondage. And when a combination of exhaustion of

* *Sharecroppers All* by Arthur Raper and Ira De A. Reid. Chapel Hill.

the land, foreign competition and rising production costs drove the price downward, New Deal subsidies helped keep the cotton farmer solvent in a system which made him grow cotton even when he was losing money.

Such subsidies cost a great deal of money, yet there was no other way out. What it really meant, however, was that the rest of the nation was subsidizing the cotton-growing South—another way of saying that Northern dollars were helping to pay slave wages and, indirectly, perpetuate racial mores closely akin to the slavery which we had fought one war to abolish.

If the cotton gin made possible the crowning of King Cotton, another invention, the mechanized cotton picker, may free the South of the economic tyranny it created. At first the change will be mainly economic but in the end it is likely to be cultural as well. If it is possible to have a new South, mechanization may bring it on with a rapidity that few anticipated, with effects as widespread and dynamic as the Industrial Revolution.

Mechanization has not progressed far enough for us to speak with certainty, but the trends are firmly established and we at least know the direction in which we are headed. The only thing open to conjecture is how far we are going and how fast we will get there. This much is inevitable: the growing and cultivation of cotton in units of less than a hundred and fifty acres will hardly be feasible. Contrast this with the old system which made necessary one sharecropper for every ten, or at most twenty, acres and we begin to see the extent of the physical change which is forthcoming. In the Delta, for example, where

149

mechanized pickers have been used in large-scale operation, labor requirements have been cut as much as eighty per cent, from one hundred and sixty man-hours per bale on a one-mule farm to twenty-eight hours with mechanized equipment.

It has been estimated that eventually it may be possible to show a profit on twelve-cent cotton, possibly even eight, where formerly a twenty-cent price usually meant a loss for any grower, large or small. At this writing cotton is about thirty-five cents and it may go higher, but eventually we are headed for the familiar "boom and bust" pattern of the past. The reason: a world cotton surplus carryover, foreign competition, local overproduction and competition from other fibers and synthetic fibers. Once we return to normal markets it seems doubtful that we can sell cotton abroad for more than ten to twelve cents a pound, even against our foreign loans. At home new markets can only be opened and old ones recaptured, if cotton sells for as low as eight cents a pound, a further indication of the importance of mechanization.

Does this point to a survival of the cotton grower, perhaps even a new period of prosperity? Probably, but only for the large operator and at a cost so high that only the most careful federal and local planning can avoid a dislocation of not only the social, political and economic structure of the South, but perhaps of the nation. The reason is simple. The mechanization of cotton, sugar cane and eventually tobacco means in plain English that within two decades as much as one-half of the Southern farm population will become surplus and will be forced off the land. By 1956 the Bureau of Farm Economics estimates that somewhere between two and three million people will be out of work, even if an expanding Southern industry should absorb new workers at its highest rate of industrial expansion, attained in the nineteen-twenties.

For those farm owners who remain, that is, those who will be in a position to work a farm of at least a hundred and fifty acres, the picture is uniformly good. It may be possible to raise the income of those farm families to a minimum of $2,500, through the growing of some grains, live stock production and, most promising of all, timber production. Such a level has never been approached in the past, even with cotton at its peak. Yet such farmers will necessarily be limited in number to those who already have the technical ability or are able to learn quickly. The low educational standards of the region and the low incidence of skilled abilities will work as a definite barrier. Cooperatives offer some hope, but we don't know enough about them yet to tell how effective they may be in taking up the slack, even with large government subsidies. At best, it appears they can only partially cushion the shock of a large-scale dislocation.

To absorb even half of those who will be thrown into unemployment will call for skilful planning, if only for the reason that the points of industrialization in the South at the present time are far away from the centers of agrarian dislocation. Bad as the short term picture may appear, however, the South will benefit to a large degree in the long run. Always in the past the best educated, the most highly skilled and the more forward looking, both white and Negro, have left the area because of limited opportunities. Mechanization is likely to put a premium on those who have these characteristics, and it will be the uneducated, the unskilled and the backward looking who will be forced to leave because there will be no place for them.

Even in the case of the Negro, it is possible that better job opportunities will exist, at least jobs which do not fall in the former "Negro" category. The trend toward larger farms and fewer farm workers may tend to urbanize large groups of Southern rural folks, subject them to the quickened tempo of city life, and make them slightly more progressive in their thinking and in their general attitudes. Labor unions will play a large part in this process and, though one cannot hope for an overnight change, eventually there will be a modification in a rural culture which has shown little or no change in the last seventy-five years.

But to return to the dislocated. As we have seen it seems unlikely that more than half of them can be absorbed into industry, nor can many hope to get together the credit and know-how necessary to hold their own in a new kind of farming, even if they band together cooperatively to rent or buy the needed mechanized equipment.

If this is true, is there any planning being done so that the process will be as orderly as possible? Preliminary planning has been spasmodic and hardly on a scale adequate to the problem. There has been some agitation for resettling dislocated families in Alaska, but the most optimistic estimates seem to show that slightly less than twenty thousand of a probable seven hundred and fifty thousand families could be absorbed in this way. Nor are there anywhere near enough farm opportunities within this country to take care of many more.

# A NEW SOUTH?

Migration seems the only answer short of a government dole. Initially the movement will be within the South, from rural to urban areas, but it will not be long before most of the dispossessed will move northward. For the time being, additional cotton subsidies to small growers and such general man-made work as can be arranged will cushion the shock, but only temporarily. The best we can hope for is an orderly withdrawal.

One thing could be done. The federal government could set up a series of dislocation centers, with trained personnel who would work closely with the United States Employment Service. After a short training period those dislocated might be systematically directed to other areas where they could be absorbed. Yet one wonders, in the light of the past record, if Congress would be willing to do even this. One thing seems certain; if we merely muddle through, the South will not be the only area affected. The stability of the whole nation may suffer.

It is probable that the whole question of race relations in the South will be affected by such a dislocation to the economy. For one thing the majority of those who migrate will be Negroes, and it is also fairly certain that they will be the first to leave the South. In fact one reputable sociologist[*] has been quoted as saying that as many as four million Negroes may leave the South in the next ten to fifteen years. Such a figure may seem high, but it is well to realize that other factors besides lack of job opportuni-

---

[*] Dr. Charles S. Johnson. Department of Social Sciences. Fisk University.

ties are involved, namely prejudice and discrimination in general. At any rate it seems safe to say that two-thirds of those who migrate will be Negroes, and by the most conservative figures this means that at least one million, two hundred and twenty-five thousand colored men and women will leave the South.

Until this actually happens we can only make a guess as to whether this will better or worsen relationships not only in the South but throughout the nation. There are already alarmists who forecast a complete breakdown of the old pattern of race relations, which, in their opinion, at least provided a racial etiquette and a set of rules governing racial conduct. Others, and this writer shares their views, feel that such a migration is more likely to lessen racial tensions and at the same time speed up the orderly breakdown of jim crow, a process which over the past five years has of itself increased in tempo. True, there is likely to be a temporary period of reaction when racists, exploiting the suffering of dislocated whites, may be able to incite racial hatred to dangerous proportions, though probably not for a prolonged length of time.

The reasons for this are fairly obvious. The difference in race relations between the border states and the deep South indicates that where the Negro population is densest, the strongest tensions exist. Since the migration will take Negroes away from those points where they are most numerous, the competition between Negroes and whites for jobs should grow less intense. In addition, one of the South's strongest arguments, the fear of political domination by Negroes, will be completely removed.

It is true that this will mean that Negro suffrage, already

well on its way in the South, will lose numerical strength but actually this is of little importance. The large majority of Negroes are more interested in the selection and election of progressive candidates than in gaining office for themselves. The urbanization of more white voters is likely to offset any temporary advantage the demagogues may gain through a large-scale migration of Negroes out of the South.

A new South, then? Possibly, once all the pieces snap together in what is now a scrambled puzzle. But even more than that, by 1956 the balance of the Negro population may be in the North, rather than the present distribution of nine millions in the South and four in the North. If this happens it could mean that those areas in the North which already have a large Negro population and are likely, through migration, to have a still larger one, might assume racial mores now peculiarly Southern. But with the techniques for adult education which we now possess this seems doubtful. It is more likely that the Mason and Dixon line will move southward below the present border states —a trend even now.

This would greatly weaken the position of the racist and bigot in the deep South. In any event his position is a precarious one now.

CHAPTER FIFTEEN

# THE PROOF OF OUR FAILURE

THE SEEDS of self-destruction are not to be found within the Negro alone; they are as deeply imbedded within ourselves. Perhaps today we can afford to delude ourselves into believing that we are working toward a solution, and any action must be gradual in order to be successful. Even tomorrow, possibly, we shall still be able to look at a new unit of Negro housing, note a report of better race relations in our large urban centers, see a more liberal South slowly emerging and find in these things great significance. But not the day after tomorrow. It is not that these things are not good or that we should be against them, but they are not in themselves a solution however badly we may want to believe that they are.

The Swedish social scientist Gunnar Myrdal* wrote: "We have two divergent and contradictory streams of thought in our culture. One, which has been called the American Creed, embraces the idea of the human personality and the nobility of man. The other tradition, and the one upon which we most frequently act, is that of racism. The subordination of people because of their color is part of our national heritage. Unless one understands the sig-

* *The American Dilemma* by Gunnar Myrdal. Harpers.

nificance of this dilemma, understands the divergent streams of thought in our national culture, understands the split in our individual souls, he cannot account for our inability to act effectively in the field of race relations."

This, of course, is the nub of the whole business, though in itself it offers no key for solution. But it is significant that we always speak in terms of race relations, rather that in terms of a permanent solution. We are ashamed that there is a Negro problem, yet we hesitate to do the thing which will show ourselves the full extent of our villainy, that is, make a full solution. To justify the fact that humanitarians could themselves force others into bondage, or at least countenance such action because of the financial gain involved, it was necessary to invent legends to prove the Negro was a problem.

Like a schizophrenic we have two sides to our personality; it is this that makes the Negro problem more than a minority problem, more than just an economic problem.

It is conceivable that if the high cost of prejudice were to be measured only in dollars and cents, or in a loss in efficiency on most levels of our economic life, it might be a luxury which we could afford. The short-term financial gain and the pleasant feeling of superiority might offset such losses, even make them seem worthwhile. But how much longer can we afford the stagnating effect on our whole culture?

Ralph Ellison, one of our better literary critics, wrote:*

---

* *Beating that Boy* by Ralph Ellison. The New Republic. October 22, 1945.

# THE HIGH COST OF PREJUDICE

"Since 1876 the race issue has been like a stave driven into the American system of values, a stave so deeply embedded in the American ethos as to render America a nation of ethical schizophrenics. Believing truly in democracy on one side of their minds, they act on the other in violation of its most sacred principles; holding that all men are created equal, they treat thirteen million Americans as though they were not.

"There are, as always, political and economic motives for this rending of values, but in terms of the ethical and the psychological, what was opportunistically labeled the 'Negro Problem' is actually a guilt problem charged with pain. Just how painful, might be judged from the ceaseless effort expended to dull its throbbing with the anesthesia of legend, myth, hypnotic ritual and narcotic modes of thinking."

We have been called a young nation but more than that we are an immature nation—culturally as well as emotionally—and part of the reason, perhaps the large part, is this very thing on which Ellison puts his finger. He goes on to say: "Indeed, the racial situation has exerted an influence upon the writer similar to an X-ray concealed in a radio. Moving about, perhaps ignoring, perhaps enjoying Jack-Rochester or a hot jazz band, he is unaware of his exposure to a force that shrivels his vital sperm. Not that he has been rendered completely sterile, but that it has caused him to produce deformed progeny: literary offspring without hearts, without brains, viscera or vision, and some even without genitalia.

"Thus it has not been its failure to depict racial matters that has determined the quality of American writing, but that the writer has formed the habit of living and thinking in a culture that is opposed to the deep thought and feeling necessary to profound art: hence its avoidance of emotions, its fears of ideas, its obsession with mere physical violence and pain, its precise and complex verbal constructions for converting goatsong into carefully modulated squeaks."

Much the same, of course, is true of many other levels of our practical as well as cultural life. The race question which is ever before us, the difference between the idea and the reality, has withered our democracy at home and abroad; we are often afraid, or unable, to act. More important, as in our condemnation of England's dealings with India, we fail to see the fallacy of our near passion for worldwide democracy and fair play when measured against our domestic policies toward our own minority groups. In our reactions we are not unlike the owners of stores on the main streets of the little towns throughout America who dress up their buildings in front with plate glass and shiny metals but leave the rest of the building the way it has been since the day it was built.

Whenever we approach the Negro question we decide to put on a new front of noble words, additional committees on race relations, larger Negro college endowments, more grants from philanthropic funds to study a problem we already know but refuse to acknowledge. Like most schizophrenics, we must atone for our failures by hiding them behind a glittering facade.

How has this actual suffering, or the guilt for having been responsible for that suffering, affected our personalities? Turning to the tools and symbols of the psychiatrist we can gain some insight into the mechanics involved. Writing on the inner purposes of the work of Richard Wright, Horace Cayton* recently had this to say: "The Negro's personality is brutalized by an unfriendly environment. This reinforces the normal insecurities he feels as a person living in this highly complex society. Such attacks on his personality lead to resentment and hatred of the white man. However, the certain knowledge that he will be discovered produces feelings of guilt for having such emotions. Fear leads to hate; but the personality recoils with an intensified and compounded fear. This is his reaction to his own brutalization, subordination and hurt. It is this vicious cycle in which the American Negro is caught and in which his personality is pulverized by an ever mounting, self-propelled rocket of emotional conflict."

But to carry Cayton's point farther, it is not only the Negro who is caught up in the vortex of emotional pulverization. The fear-hate-fear complex of the Negro is matched by the guilt-hate-fear complex of most whites. The guilt, of course, is the fact that the Negro is the proof of our failure in democracy, the main reason for the schizophrenia which has become a part of our collective personality. As for the hate, we always hate that which shows us up for a fraud. The fear, and it seems to us a very real fear, is that of retribution, that if the controls are relaxed Negroes will retaliate and punish us, just as we would do if the positions were reversed. Even if true this would be

---

* *Frightened Children of Frightened Parents* by Horace R. Cayton. Twice-a-Year. Issue of 1945.

---

pure nonsense; Negroes are outnumbered ten to one and we have all the means of offensive techniques.

This feeling of guilt-fear-hate appears on many levels, just as the fear-hate-fear of Negroes is not limited to the Bigger Thomas of Richard Wright or the Bob Jones of Chester B. Himes. It may be so deeply embedded in the subconscious that it may never appear, or it may erupt suddenly into the violence of a lynch mob or a race riot. Probably it is one of the basic reasons why we cling so stubbornly to our policies of segregation which, although mainly economic on the surface as we have seen, may be below that the desire of guilty persons to put away from sight that which reminds them of their guilt. We can never really do this, save perhaps by colonization, but segregation is the nearest approximation.

To those who may think this far fetched, how else can one explain racial dreams, the hidden fear of a woman who awakes in the night feeling that a Negro has entered her room, the child who has fantasies in which a very black demon keeps chasing him, even the man, and he is not uncommon, who feels himself sexually ineffective because of the myths he has heard concerning the virity of black savages. Even whites who have never lived near Negroes or had any contacts with them react to the legends they have absorbed with childhood, the stereotypes they have read about in books, heard on the radio or seen in the moving pictures. The white Southerner hopes for salvation from the individual Negro whom the regional mores allow him to befriend; the Northern white, in his abstract justice for the group at large, hopes to atone for the wrongs he has done the individual.

161

# THE HIGH COST OF PREJUDICE

All these fears and doubts, all this mumbo-jumbo of half-remembered legends and myths, combine to make the so-called Negro problem somewhat apart from other minority problems which are not complicated by color. Three generations of Americans, white and Negro, have been corroded by the process of legal and sanctioned racial prejudice and discrimination. It has made Negroes do those very things which most hurt their cause, merely because their frustration made it impossible for them to stop for fear of losing the will to fight back, a state not too different from the battle fatigue of the soldier. In whites this is the same frustration that the racist and the bigot use to start lynchings and riots. It is a psychosis, and we must recognize it as such.

We are a sick people because of this schism in our lives, so much so that we will not even admit it to ourselves. To justify our guilt we say that Negroes are ignorant, but deny them adequate educational facilities; that Negroes are criminals, then segregate them in slums which produce more crime; that Negroes are lazy and shiftless, while shutting them off from all but the most menial jobs; and that their family life is irregular, only to hold back the human dignity that makes for permanent relationships. If we did not do this our failure would be complete, obvious even to ourselves.

If we would solve the Negro problem, first we must make sure that we really want to solve it, not merely ease the tensions which are its outer manifestations. It is our problem and not the Negro's. We originated it, first for financial gain and then to relieve the guilt which was that gain measured against our humanitarian impulses. Since it has become an integral part of our culture, it will not be easy to root out. This is not, however, to say that it is by any means insoluble. It is at bottom an economic problem, and no economic problem is insoluble, even when complicated by moral, ethical and psychological overtones. But it cannot be solved on one level without being at the same time attacked on the other.

We must find some method of facing ourselves squarely —if not individually, then through some sort of collective action, be it mass psychiatry, the ferment of social change, philosophy, or, perhaps easiest, the democratic process. But it must be an accelerated process, for time is running out. We must also clearly understand that we have already gone through the initial phase: there has been enough agitation. We are aware of the problem's existence and the need for some solution. In other words we now have a strategy and must pass on to those tactics which will best put that strategy into social action. Further agitation, merely for the sake of agitation, can no longer have a positive effect, only a negative one.

Next, we must face one issue head on, and that is the issue of segregation. Not to take action against it is suicide, for within the framework of segregation there is no possible solution—economic, moral, or practical. Jobs, better schools, even the ballot, are needs but can never be ends under such a policy. Even if all were realized, there would still be a Negro problem—perhaps a lesser one but nevertheless the same basic problem. If, however, we work rapidly, firmly and intelligently towards the orderly breakdown of segregation, we may still have a problem but it

163

will no longer be a Negro problem alone. It may still be an economic problem or even one among many minority problems, but it can be dealt with by the tools of social pressure.

The tactics at our command are many and we must utilize them all—legal and legislative action, social change, and the pressures instituted by the agencies of the community; the school, the church, social agencies, labor unions and political groups. This action cannot be gradual in the old accepted sense; to move slowly now may be not to move at all.

The Negro has been called the barometer of democracy, but he is far more than that. So long as we have no solution for the Negro problem, we have no solution for any minority problem. And so long as our false concepts of racial superiority continue, the Negro can never be an American, but more than that, Americans can never be free men.

# CHECK LIST FOR FURTHER READING

THE FOLLOWING listing is far from being all-inclusive, but merely contains those books which I have found sound and helpful over the past five or six years. A most complete bibliography on race literature was recently published by the Rosenwald Fund and may be obtained by writing to 4901 Ellis Avenue, Chicago, Illinois. The magazines *Common Ground, The Negro Digest,* and before it ceased publication, *South Today,* carry an unusually high percentage of valuable material, as do the various Negro newspapers. The pamphlets put out by the Public Affairs Committee are also worth careful consideration.

Aptheker, Herbert. *Essays in the History of the American Negro.* International.
Aptheker, Herbert. *American Negro Slave Revolts.* Columbia University Press.
Attaway, William. *Blood on the Forge.* Doubleday.
Benedict, Ruth. *Race, Science and Politics.* Viking.
Bontemps, Arna and Conroy, Jack. *They Seek a City.* Doubleday.
Botkin, B. A. *Lay My Burden Down.* University of Chicago Press.
Brown, Davis and Lee. *The Negro Caravan.* Dryden Press.
Buckmaster, Henrietta. *Let My People Go.* Harpers.
Carter, Hodding. *The Winds of Fear.* Farrar and Rinehart.
Cash, W. L. *The Mind of the South.* Knopf.
Cayton, Horace R. and Mitchell, G. S. *Black Workers and the New Unions.* Chapel Hill.

# CHECK LIST FOR FURTHER READING

Cayton, Horace R. and St. Clair Drake. *Black Metropolis.* Harcourt, Brace.

Conrad, Earl. *Harriet Tubman.* The Associated Publishers.

Cook, Fannie. *Mrs. Palmer's Honey.* Doubleday.

Cox, Oliver. *Caste, Class and Race.* Doubleday.

Cullen, Countee. *Caroling Dusk.* Harpers.

Davis, Gardner and Gardner. *Deep South.* University of Chicago Press.

Ehrlich, Leonard. *God's Angry Man.* Simon and Schuster.

Embree, Edwin. *Brown Americans.* Viking.

Embree, Edwin. *13 Against the Odds.* Viking.

Fast, Howard. *Freedom Road.* Duell, Sloan and Pearce.

Frazier, E. Franklin. *The Negro Family in Chicago.* University of Chicago Press.

Frazier, E. Franklin. *The Negro Family in the United States.* University of Chicago Press.

Fuller, Edmund. *A Star Pointed North.* Harpers.

Gallagher, Buell. *Color and Conscience.* Harpers.

Graham, Shirley. *There Was Once a Slave.* Messner.

Halsey, Margaret. *Color Blind.* Simon and Schuster.

Herskovits, Melville J. *The American Negro.* Knopf.

Herskovits, Melville J. *The Myth of the Negro Past.* Harpers.

Himes, Chester B. *If He Hollers Let Him Go.* Doubleday.

Holt, Rackham. *George Washington Carver.* Doubleday.

Hughes, Langston. *Not Without Laughter.* Knopf.

Hughes, Langston. *The Big Sea.* Knopf.

Hughes, Langston. *The Ways of White Folks.* Knopf.

Hurston, Zora Neale. *Mules and Men.* Lippincott.

Johnson, Charles S. *The Negro College Graduate.* Chapel Hill.

Johnson, Charles S. *Patterns of Negro Segregation.* Harpers.

Johnson, James Weldon. *Along This Way.* Viking.

Johnson, James Weldon. *Black Manhattan.* Knopf.

# CHECK LIST FOR FURTHER READING

Kennedy, Stetson. *Southern Exposure*. Doubleday.

Klineburg, Otto. *Characteristics of the American Negro*. Harpers.

Logan, Rayford W. and others. *What the Negro Wants*. Chapel Hill.

Montagu, Ashley. *Man's Most Dangerous Fallacy*. University of Columbia Press.

Moon, Bucklin. *The Darker Brother*. Doubleday.

Moon, Bucklin. *Primer for White Folks*. Doubleday.

Murray, Florence. *The Negro Handbook*. Wynn.

Myrdal, Gunnar. *An American Dilemma*. Harpers.

Northrup, Herbert R. *Organized Labor and the Negro*. Harpers.

Ottley, Roi. *New World A-coming*. Houghton Mifflin.

Petry, Ann. *The Street*. Houghton Mifflin.

Powdermaker, Hortense. *After Freedom*. Viking.

Raper, Arthur and Ira De A. Reid. *Sharecroppers All*. Chapel Hill.

Raper, Arthur. *Preface to Peasantry*. Chapel Hill.

Raper, Arthur. *The Tragedy of Lynching*. Chapel Hill.

Schoenfields, Seymour J. *The Negro in the Armed Forces*. The Associated Publishers.

Smith, Lillian. *Strange Fruit*. Reynal and Hitchcock.

Stenger, Wallace. *One Nation*. Houghton Mifflin.

Stern, Philip Van Doren. *The Drums of Morning*. Doubleday.

Sterner, Richard. *The Negro's Share*. Harpers.

Tannenbaum, Frank. *Slave and Citizen*. Knopf.

Virginia Writers Project. *The Negro in Virginia*. Hastings House.

Walker, Margaret. *For My People*. Yale University Press.

Watkins, Sylvester C. *An Anthology of American Negro Literature*. Modern Library.

Weaver, Robert. *Negro Labor*. Harcourt, Brace.

167

# CHECK LIST FOR FURTHER READING

White, Walter. *A Rising Wind*. Doubleday.

White, Walter. *Rope and Faggot*. Knopf.

Williams, Eric. *Capitalism and Slavery*. Chapel Hill.

Woodson, Carter G. *The Negro in Our History*. The Associated Publishers.

Wright, Richard. *Black Boy*. Harpers.

Wright, Richard. *Native Son*. Harpers.

Wright, Richard. *12 Million Black Voices*. Viking.

Wright, Richard. *Uncle Tom's Children*. Harpers.